P9-BJK-250

Anxiety & Depression
FOR
DUMMIES®
POCKET EDITION

by Laura L. Smith, PhD and Charles H. Elliott, PhD

Look for Pocket Editions on these other topics:

Allergies For Dummies, Pocket Edition
Asthma For Dummies, Pocket Edition
Diabetes For Dummies, Pocket Edition
Dieting For Dummies, Pocket Edition
Heart Disease For Dummies, Pocket Edition
High Blood Pressure For Dummies, Pocket Edition
Menopause For Dummies, Pocket Edition
Migraines For Dummies, Pocket Edition

WILEY

Wiley Publishing, Inc.

Anxiety & Depression For Dummies® Pocket Edition

Published by
Wiley Publishing, Inc.
111 River St.
Hoboken, NJ 07030-5774
www.wiley.com

For general information on our other products and services, please contact our Customer Care Department within the U.S. at 800-762-2974, outside the U.S. at 317-572-3993, or fax 317-572-4002.

For technical support, please visit www.wiley.com/techsupport.

Wiley also publishes its books in a variety of electronic formats. Some content that appears in print may not be available in electronic books.

Library of Congress Control Number: 2005936641

ISBN-13: 978-0-471-79239-0

ISBN-10: 0-471-79239-X

Manufactured in the United States of America

10 9 8 7 6 5 4 3 2 1

1O/QZ/QR/QW/IN

Publisher's Acknowledgments

Project Editor: Georgette Beatty
Copy Editor: Melissa Wiley
Composition Services: Indianapolis Composition Services Department
Cover Photo: © The Image Bank/Alain Daussin

Table of Contents

● ●

Introduction

• •

Today's world gives us plenty to worry about and always has. But just as we don't want to become victims of terror, we can't let ourselves become victims of anxiety. Anxiety clouds our thinking and weakens our resolve to live life to the fullest. We realize that some anxiety is realistic and inescapable, yet we can keep it from dominating our lives. Even under duress, we can preserve a degree of serenity; we can hold on to our humanity, vigor, and zest for life.

Theories also abound concerning the alarming increase in depression today. But regardless of the cause, this scourge robs its victims of happiness, joy, and the capacity to give and receive love. The good news is that more weapons exist for defeating depression than ever before. Clinicians have devised new psychotherapies verified as effective in treating depression and preventing relapse. Furthermore, science is beginning to understand the delicate relationship between mood and brain chemistry. Medications that target specific chemicals provide important additional tools for the alleviation of depression. The vast majority of people no longer need to suffer with long-standing, intractable depression.

About This Book

We're keenly aware of the pain and profound despair you may be experiencing. Your sense of humor is likely depleted. With this book, we attempt to lighten exquisitely somber subjects with tidbits of humor. Some of you may take offense with our attempts or even feel diminished or discounted by this decision.

We can understand that reaction. At the same time, your long-term goals need to include rediscovering laughter. Thus, we hope you can try to take our occasional use of wit in the manner we intend it — as another way to help you lift yourself out of the fog of anxiety and depression.

In addition, we realize that the title *Anxiety & Depression For Dummies* may seem offensive to some, especially because when people are depressed, they're prone to make negative, personalized interpretations. However, we assure you that the content of this book is as serious and in-depth as any book on anxiety and depression. The *For Dummies* format simply enables us to present important material in easily digestible segments. We leave it up to you to determine if we succeed in doing so.

Unlike most books, you don't have to start on page 1 and read straight through. Use the Table of Contents to pick and choose what you want to read.

Conventions Used in This Book

We avoid the use of professional jargon as much as possible. When we occasionally find it necessary to use a technical term, we clearly define the term.

We also include numerous stories to illustrate the information and techniques we present. The people you read about aren't real; however, they represent composites of the many wonderful people we've known and worked with over the years. We bold the name of each character the first time it appears to alert you to the fact that we're telling a story.

Finally, if you're reading this book because you want help in defeating your own depression, we recommend that you purchase a spiral notebook. Use your notebook to write out the exercises we present throughout the book. We call these exercises Antidepression Tools and highlight them with an icon. Use your notebook often and reread what you've written from time to time.

What You're Not to Read

Not only do you not have to read each and every chapter in order or at all, you don't have to read each and every icon or aside. We try to give you plenty of current information and facts about anxiety and depression. Some may not interest you — so don't get too anxious about skipping around.

Foolish Assumptions

We assume, probably foolishly, that you or someone you love suffers from some type of problem with anxiety, worry, or depression. We also hope that you want information to help tame tension and overcome anxiety or to banish depression from your life. Finally, we imagine you're curious about a variety of helpful strategies that can fit your lifestyle and personality.

Icons Used in This Book

 This icon points out an exercise you can use to hammer away at or discover more about your depression.

 This icon represents a tip for getting rid of anxiety.

Please read text with this icon for critical information.

 This icon alerts you to important insights or clarifications.

 This icon appears when you need to be careful or seek professional help.

Where to Go from Here

Most books are written so that you have to start on page 1 and read straight through. But we wrote this book so that you can use the Table of Contents to pick and choose what you want to read based on your individual interests. Don't worry too much about reading chapters in any particular order. Read whatever chapters apply to your situation.

If you want even more information on anxiety and depression, check out the full-size versions of *Overcoming Anxiety For Dummies* and *Depression For Dummies* — simply head to your local book seller or go to www.dummies.com!

Chapter 1

Examining Different Types of Anxiety

* *

* *

Anxiety comes in various forms. The word *anxious* is a derivative of the Latin word *angere,* meaning to strangle or choke. A sense of choking or tightening in the throat or chest is a common symptom of anxiety. However, anxiety also involves symptoms such as sweating, trembling, nausea, and a racing heartbeat; anxiety may also involve fears — fear of losing control and fear of illness or dying. In addition, people with excessive anxiety avoid various situations, people, animals, or objects to an unnecessary degree. Psychologists and psychiatrists have compiled a list of seven major categories of anxiety disorders as follows:

- Generalized Anxiety Disorder (GAD)
- Social Phobia
- Panic Disorder
- Agoraphobia
- Specific Phobia
- Post-Traumatic Stress Disorder (PTSD)
- Obsessive-Compulsive Disorder (OCD)

In this chapter, we describe the signs and indications of each of the major types of anxiety disorders. Medical students are renowned for thinking they have developed every new disease they study. Readers of psychology books sometimes do the same thing. Don't freak out if you or someone you love experiences some of these symptoms. Almost everyone has a few.

You don't need a full-blown diagnosis to feel that you have some trouble with anxiety. Many people have more anxiety than they want but don't completely fit the category of having an official anxiety disorder.

 Only a mental health professional can tell you for certain what type of anxiety you have, because various disorders can look similar (see Chapter 2).

Although we provide the major signs and symptoms of each type of anxiety so that you can get a general idea of what category your anxiety may fall under, to really understand where your particular anxiety fits, you need to see a professional (see Chapter 8).

Generalized Anxiety Disorder: The Common Cold of Anxiety

Some people refer to *Generalized Anxiety Disorder* as the common cold of anxiety disorders. Generalized Anxiety Disorder, also known as GAD, afflicts more people throughout the world than any other anxiety disorder. So if you or a loved one has it, you're in good company. GAD involves a long-lasting, almost constant state of tension and worry. Realistic worries don't mean you have GAD. For example, if you worry about money and you just lost your job, you don't have GAD — you have a real-life problem. But if you constantly worry about money and your name is Bill Gates, you just may have GAD!

You may have GAD if your anxiety has shown up almost every day for the last six months. You try to stop worrying, but you just can't, *and* you frequently experience a number of the following problems:

✔ You feel restless, often irritable, on edge, fidgety, or keyed up.

✔ You get tired easily.

✔ Your muscles feel tense, especially in your back, neck, or shoulders.

✔ You have difficulty concentrating, falling asleep, or staying asleep.

Not everyone experiences anxiety in exactly the same way, which is why only a professional can actually make a diagnosis. Some people complain about other problems, such as twitching, trembling, shortness of breath, sweating, dry mouth, stomach upset, feeling shaky, being easily startled, and having difficulty swallowing, and fail to realize that they actually suffer from GAD.

The following profile offers an example of what GAD is all about.

In a subway, **Brian** taps his foot nervously. He arches his back to stretch his tight shoulder muscles and checks his watch, fretting that he might arrive at work three or four minutes late. He hates showing up late. He didn't sleep much last night because his thoughts about presenting the design for the new Alaska resort project invaded his sleep; one preoccupation or another usually disturbs Brian's sleep. He struggles to concentrate on the newspaper he's holding and realizes that he can't remember what he just read.

When Brian gets to work, he snaps at his new assistant. After he loses his temper at her, he feels immediate remorse and scolds himself, increasing his anxiety further. His office mates often tell him to chill out. His performance has always exceeded his employer's expectations, so he really has no reason to worry about his job. But he does. Brian suffers from *Generalized Anxiety Disorder.*

Social Phobia: Avoiding People

People with *Social Phobia* fear exposure to public scrutiny. They frequently dread performing, speaking, going to parties, meeting new people, entering groups, using the telephone, writing a check in front of others, eating in public, and/or interacting with those in authority. They see these situations as painful, because they expect to receive humiliating or shameful judgments from others. Social phobics

believe that they're somehow defective and inade-
quate; thus, they assume they'll bungle their lines,
spill their drinks, shake hands with clammy palms,
or commit any number of social *faux pas* and thus
embarrass themselves.

Everyone feels uncomfortable or nervous from
time to time, especially in new situations. For
example, if you've been experiencing social fears
for less than six months, you may not have
Social Phobia. A short-term fear of socializing
may be a temporary reaction to a new stress —
moving to a new neighborhood or getting a new
job. However, you may have Social Phobia if you
experience the following symptoms for a pro-
longed period of time:

✔ You fear situations with unfamiliar people or
   where you might be observed or evaluated in
   some way.

✔ When forced into an uncomfortable social situation, your anxiety increases powerfully. For
   example, if you fear public speaking, your voice
   shakes, and your knees tremble the moment
   that you start to talk.

✔ You realize that your fear is greater than the situation really warrants. For example, if you fear
   meeting new people, logically you know nothing
   horrible will happen, but tidal waves of adrenaline and fearful anticipation course through
   your veins.

✔ You avoid fearful situations as much as you can
   or endure them only with great distress.

Check out the following prime example of a social
phobic and see if any of it seems familiar.

Quinton, a 35-year-old eligible bachelor, wants a serious relationship. Women consider him fairly attractive, a good dresser, and they know he has a high-paying job. Quinton's friends invite him to parties and other social events in an effort to set him up. Unfortunately, he detests the idea of going; on the day after Christmas, he starts dreading the New Year's Eve party. In his mind, Quinton conjures up a number of good excuses for backing out. However, his desire to meet potential dates eventually wins. He runs scenes of meeting women over and over in his mind. Each time that he imagines one of these scenes, he feels intense, anxious anticipation. He berates himself, realizing that his fear is absurd, but feels powerless to do anything about it.

The afternoon of the party, he spends hours getting ready and has no appetite. When Quinton arrives, he immediately heads to the bar to quell his mounting anxiety. His hands shake as he picks up his first drink. Quickly downing the drink, he orders more in hopes of numbing his emotions. After an hour of nonstop drinking, he feels much braver. He interrupts a cluster of attractive women and spews out a string of jokes that he memorized for the occasion. Then he approaches various women throughout the night, sometimes making flirtatious, suggestive comments. He doesn't get far, but he feels good about his performance.

The next day Quinton awakes in an unfamiliar bedroom, not remembering the end of the evening. His buddy pokes his head into the room and says, "You were so far gone last night that we took your keys and put you to bed. Do you remember what happened?" Quinton shakes his head no, his face flush with embarrassment. His buddy continues, "Well, I hate to tell you this, but you were making some pretty on-the-edge come-ons to Brenda. She felt really turned off. Her brother almost lost it with you, and you were ready to fight. All in all, it wasn't a pretty sight."

The paradox of Social Phobia

Because of their expectation and fear of experiencing humiliation, people with Social Phobia withdraw and avoid social situations whenever possible. When forced into such encounters, they inhibit their actions in order to avoid saying or doing something that they believe will be seen as stupid. They often avoid eye contact, stand alone, add little to conversations, and generally look stiff.

Unfortunately, their fear of expressing themselves sometimes makes social phobics appear unfriendly, cold, distant, and/or self-centered. Social phobics actually experience intense fear in social circumstances and react with surprise to feedback that they seem self-centered and unfriendly. Sometimes they realize that others perceive them as unfriendly, which only fuels their phobia and convinces them that people won't like them and that they don't know how to interact successfully. In other words, a vicious cycle ensues — the more that social phobics try to avoid negative reactions, the more that others react negatively.

Quinton has Social Phobia. Drug and alcohol abuse often accompany Social Phobia. Perhaps you can see why.

Feeling Panicky

Of course, everyone feels a little panicked from time to time. People often say they feel panicked about an upcoming deadline, an impending presentation, or planning a party. You're likely to hear the term *panicked* to describe concerns about rather mundane events.

But people who suffer from *Panic Disorders* are talking about different phenomena entirely. They have periods of stunningly intense fear and anxiety. If you've never had a panic attack, we don't recommend it. The attacks usually last about ten minutes, and many people who have them fully believe that they will die during the attack. Not exactly the best ten minutes of their lives. Panic attacks normally include a range of robust, attention-grabbing symptoms, such as

- ✓ Irregular, rapid, or pounding heartbeat
- ✓ Perspiring
- ✓ A sense of choking, suffocation, or shortness of breath
- ✓ Vertigo or lightheadedness
- ✓ Pain or other discomfort in the chest
- ✓ Feeling that events are unreal or a sense of detachment from yourself
- ✓ Numbness or tingling
- ✓ Hot or cold flashes
- ✓ Fearing that you will die, though without basis in fact
- ✓ Stomach nausea or upset
- ✓ Jitteriness or trembling
- ✓ Thoughts of going insane or completely losing control

Professionals generally agree that in order to have a full-blown Panic Disorder, panic attacks must occur more than once. People with Panic Disorder worry about when the next panic attack will come and whether they'll lose control and embarrass themselves. Finally, they usually start changing their lives by avoiding certain places or activities.

Panic attacks begin with an event that triggers some kind of sensation, such as physical exertion or normal variations in physiological reactions. This triggering event induces physiological responses such as increased levels of adrenaline. No problem so far.

But the otherwise normal process goes awry at the next step — when the person who suffers from panic attacks misinterprets the meaning of the physical symptoms. Rather than viewing it as a normal event, the person with Panic Disorder sees it as a signal that something dangerous is happening, such as a heart attack or stroke. That interpretation causes escalating fear and thus more physical arousal. In other words, it becomes a vicious cycle. Fortunately, the body can sustain such heightened physical responses only for a while before it eventually calms down.

The good news: Many people have a single panic attack and never have another one. So don't panic if you have a panic attack.

Maria's story is a good example of a one-time panic attack.

Maria left the hospital after visiting her next-door neighbor. She still can't believe he had a heart attack at the age of 42. Maria, never one to worry about her health, ponders the fact that she just reached her 46th birthday. She resolves to lose that extra 20 pounds and to start exercising.

On her third visit to the gym, she sets the treadmill to a level six. Almost immediately, her heart rate accelerates rapidly. Alarmed, she decreases the level to three. She starts taking rapid, shallow breaths but feels she can't get enough air. Reducing the level further doesn't seem to help. She stops the treadmill and goes to the locker room. Sweating profusely and feeling nauseous, she finds an empty dressing cubicle. She sits down and thinks maybe she just overdid the treadmill a little. But the symptoms intensify and her chest tightens. She wants to scream but can't get enough air. She's sure that she'll pass out and hopes someone will find her before she dies. She hears someone and weakly calls for help. An ambulance whisks her to a nearby emergency room while she prays that she'll live through her heart attack.

At the emergency room, Maria's symptoms subside, and the doctor comes in to explain the results of her examination. He says that she's apparently experienced a panic attack and inquires about what may have set it off. She explains that she was exercising due to concerns about her weight and health, and she mentions her neighbor's heart attack.

Help! I'm dying!

Panic attack symptoms, such as chest pain, shortness of breath, nausea, and intense fear, often mimic heart attacks. Alarmed, people who experience these terrifying episodes take off in the direction of the nearest emergency room. Then, after numerous tests come back negative, overworked doctors tell the victim of a panic attack in so many words, "It's all in your head." Unbelieving panic attack patients are sure that something was missed. The next time an attack occurs, panic attack victims are likely to return to the ER for another opinion — again and again. The repeat visits frustrate people with panic attacks as well as ER staff. However, a simple 20- or 30-minute psychological intervention in the emergency room decreases the repeat visits dramatically. What is the intervention? It can be just providing education about what the disorder is all about and describing a few deep relaxation techniques to try out when panic hits.

"Ah, that explains it," the doctor reassures her. "Your concerns about health made you hypersensitive to any bodily symptom. When your heart rate naturally increased on the treadmill, you became alarmed. That fear caused your body to produce more adrenaline, which in turn created more symptoms. The more symptoms you had, the more that your fear and adrenaline increased. Knowing how this works may help you; hopefully, in the future, your body's normal physical variations won't frighten you. Your heart's in great shape. I recommend that you go back to exercising, but just increase it slowly over time without sudden jumps in intensity. Also, you might try some simple relaxation techniques; I'll have the nurse come in and tell you about those. I have every reason to believe that you won't have another episode like this one. Finally, you may want to read *Overcoming Anxiety For Dummies* by Charles Elliott and Laura Smith (Wiley Publishing, Inc.); it's a great book!"

Maria doesn't have a diagnosis of Panic Disorder because she hasn't experienced more than one attack, and she may never have an attack again. If she believes the doctor and takes his advice, the next time that her heart races, she probably won't get so scared. She may even use the relaxation techniques that the nurse explained to her.

If you worry that you have a Panic Disorder, remember that it can be treated.

The Panic Companion: Agoraphobia

Somewhere around half of those with a Panic Disorder have an accompanying problem: *Agoraphobia*. Unlike most fears or phobias, this strange disorder usually

begins in adulthood. Individuals with Agoraphobia
live in terror of being trapped. In addition, they worry
about having a panic attack, throwing up, or having
diarrhea in public. They desperately avoid situations
from which they can't readily escape, and they also
fear places where help might not be readily forthcom-
ing should they need it. The agoraphobic may start
with one fear, such as being in a crowd, but in many
cases the feared situations multiply to the point that
the person fears even leaving home.

When Agoraphobia combines with Panic Disorder,
individuals fear any situation in which they might
have an attack. As Agoraphobia teams up with Panic
Disorder, the double-barreled fears of not getting help
and horror at the idea of feeling entombed with no
way out frequently lead to paralyzing isolation.

You or someone you love may have Agoraphobia if

   ✔ You worry about being somewhere you can't get
      out of or can't get help from in case something
      bad happens, like a panic attack.

   ✔ You tremble over everyday things like leaving
      home, being in large groups of people, or
      traveling.

   ✔ Because of your anxiety, you avoid the places
      you fear so much that it takes over your life,
      and you become a prisoner of your fear.

 You may have concerns about feeling trapped
or have anxiety about crowds and leaving home.
Many people do. But if your life goes on without
major changes or constraints, you're probably
not agoraphobic.

Nevertheless, you could still have problems with your
fears in this area, or maybe not. For example, you may
quake at the thought of entering large sports stadiums.
You see images of stampeding crowds pushing and

shoving, causing you to fall over the railings, landing below, only to be trampled by the mob as you cry out. If so, you could live an entire blissful life avoiding sports stadiums. Thus, your fears don't bother you much. But if you love watching live sports events, or you just got a job as a sports reporter, this fear could be *really bad*.

Patricia's story, which follows, demonstrates the overwhelming anxiety that often traps agoraphobics.

Patricia celebrates her 40th birthday without having experienced significant emotional problems. She'd gone through the usual bumps in the road of life, like losing a parent, having a child with a learning disability, and undergoing a divorce ten years earlier. She prides herself on being able to cope with whatever cards life deals her.

Lately, she notices that she stresses when she shops at the mall. She needs to pick up a birthday present but doesn't want to go because the mall is especially crowded on weekends. She finally finds a parking spot at the very end of a row. Her sweaty hands leave a smudge on the revolving glass door. She feels as though the crowd of shoppers is crushing in on her, and Patricia feels trapped. She's so scared that she can't bring herself to buy the present and flees the store.

Over the next few months, her fears spread. Although it started at the mall, fear and anxiety now overwhelm her in crowded grocery stores as well. Later, she can no longer cope when she's simply driving in traffic. Patricia suffers from Agoraphobia. If not treated, Patricia could end up housebound.

Many times, panic, Agoraphobia, and anxiety strike people who are otherwise devoid of serious, deep-seated emotional problems. So if you suffer from anxiety, it doesn't necessarily mean you need years of psychotherapy.

Specific Phobia: Spiders, Snakes, and Other Scary Things

Many fears appear to be hard-wired into the human brain. Cave men and women had good reasons to fear snakes, strangers, heights, darkness, open spaces, and the sight of blood — snakes could be poisonous, strangers could be enemies, a person could fall from a height, darkness could harbor unknown hazards, open spaces could leave a primitive tribe vulnerable to attack from all sides, and the sight of blood could signal a crisis, even potential death. Fear inspired caution and avoidance of harm. Those with these fears had a better chance of survival than the naively brave.

That's why many of the most common fears today reflect the dangers of the world thousands of years ago. Even today, it makes sense to cautiously identify a spider before you pick it up. However, sometimes fears rise to a disabling level. You may have a *Specific Phobia* if

- ✔ You have an exaggerated fear of a specific situation or object.

- ✔ When you're in fearful situations, you experience excessive anxiety immediately. Your anxiety may include sweating, a rapid heartbeat, a desire to flee, tightness in the chest or throat, or images of something awful happening.

- ✔ You know the fear is unreasonable. On the other hand, kids with Specific Phobias don't always know that their phobia is unreasonable. For example, they may really think that *all* dogs bite.

- ✔ You avoid your feared object or situation as much as you possibly can.

> ✔ Because your fear is so intense, you go so far as to change your day-to-day behavior at work, at home, or in relationships. Thus, your fear inconveniences you and perhaps others, and it restricts your life.

Almost two-thirds of people fear one thing or another. For example, I, Laura Smith (one of the authors of this book), hate bugs. Whenever a cricket is in the house, I avoid it or get someone else to dispose of it. One year, I had an office in an old building. Every morning, dead roaches littered the floor. I devised ways of getting them out of my office using a huge wad of paper towels. If instead I had quit my job because of the bugs, I would have had a diagnosis of Specific Phobia. But my fears don't significantly interfere with my life. You, like me, may have an excessive fear of something. That doesn't mean that you have a Specific Phobia in the diagnosable sense, as long as it doesn't disrupt your life in a major way. And you may or may not want to do something about it. In case you're wondering, I don't particularly mind the fact that bugs gross me out; I intend to live out my entire life in this manner and have no desire to work on this problem.

In contrast, the following description of Ted's life is a prime picture of what someone with a Specific Phobia goes through.

Ted trudges up eight flights of stairs each morning to get to his office and tells everyone that he loves the exercise. When Ted passes the elevators on the way to the stairwell, his heart pounds, and he feels a sense of doom. Ted envisions being boxed inside the elevator; the doors slide shut, and there's no escape. In his mind, the elevator box rises on rusty cables, makes sudden jerks up and down, falls freely, and crashes into the basement.

Ted has never experienced anything like his fantasy, nor has anyone he knows. Ted never liked elevators, but he didn't start avoiding them until the past few years. It seems that the longer he stays away from riding them, the stronger his fear grows. He used to feel okay on escalators, but now he finds himself avoiding those as well. Several weeks ago at the airport, he had no alternative but to take the escalator. He managed to get on but became so frightened that he had to sit down for a while after he reached the second floor.

One afternoon, Ted rushes down the stairs after work, running late for an appointment. He slips and falls, breaking his leg. Now in a cast, Ted faces the challenge of his life. Ted has a Specific Phobia.

Post-Traumatic Stress Disorder: Feeling the Aftermath

Tragically, war, rape, terror, crashes, brutality, torture, and natural disasters are a part of life. You or someone you know may have experienced one of life's traumas. No one knows why for sure, but some people seem to recover from these events without disabling symptoms. However, many others suffer considerably after their tragedy, sometimes for a lifetime.

More often than not, trauma causes at least a few uncomfortable emotional and/or physical reactions for a while. These responses can show up immediately after the disaster, or sometimes they emerge years later. These symptoms are the way that the body and mind deal with and process what happened. If an extremely unfortunate event occurs, it's normal to react strongly.

The diagnosis of *Post-Traumatic Stress Disorder* (PTSD) is complicated. If you suspect that you may have it, you should seek professional help. On the other hand, you may realize that you have a few of the following symptoms but not the full diagnosis. If so, and if your problem feels mild and doesn't interfere with your life, you may want to try working on the difficulty on your own for a while. But seek help if you don't feel better.

You may have PTSD if you personally experienced or witnessed an event that you perceived as potentially life threatening or as causing serious injury or you discovered that someone close to you experienced such an event. If your response included terror, horror, or helplessness, *three types of problems* also occur if you have PTSD:

- ✔ You *relive* the event in one or more ways, such as having unwanted memories or flashbacks during the day or in your dreams, feeling the trauma is happening again, and experiencing physical or emotional reactions when reminded of the event.

- ✔ You *avoid* anything that reminds you of the trauma and try to suppress or numb your feelings in several ways, such as trying to block out thinking or talking about the event, staying away from people or places that remind you of the trauma, losing interest in life or feeling distant from people, sensing somehow that you don't have a long future, and feeling numb or detached.

- ✔ You feel *on guard and stirred up* in several ways, such as becoming startled more easily, losing your temper quickly and feeling irritable, being unable to concentrate as well as before, and sleeping fitfully.

What's it like to live with PTSD? For Wayne, it's a constant struggle.

Wayne retired from the military at age 40 as a full colonel. Before retirement, the years following the Gulf War were a struggle for Wayne. He slept poorly, and nightmares frequently awakened him; he lost his temper easily, and he felt detached from life.

Wayne assumed his problems all stemmed from issues related to the military: his work hours, frequent separations from his family, numerous cross-country moves, and the intense pressure for promotions. He looked forward to retirement and a less stressful lifestyle. He promised his wife and children that his first goal was to spend more time with them.

But Wayne finds retirement less rewarding than he'd hoped. He continues to have trouble sleeping. He tries to fulfill his promise to his family but just can't muster any enthusiasm for their activities. He doesn't find anything to look forward to, and his distance from his family grows. He continues to feel irritable and jumpy. After six months of retirement, Wayne's wife insists they get marital counseling.

In taking their history, the psychologist asks Wayne about his Gulf War experience. Wayne says he doesn't want to talk about it, which is how he handles the disturbing memories of the war. Wayne's answer tips the psychologist off to Wayne's problem: Wayne has PTSD.

Obsessive-Compulsive Disorder: Over and Over Again

Obsessive-Compulsive Disorder (OCD) wreaks incredible havoc on people's lives, because OCD frustrates and confuses not only the people afflicted with it but their families and loved ones as well. If untreated,

OCD is likely to last a lifetime. Even with treatment, symptoms often recur. That's the bad news. Thankfully, effective treatments are available.

A person with OCD may exhibit behaviors that include an obsession or a compulsion or both. So what are obsessions versus compulsions?

Obsessions are unwelcome repetitive images, impulses, or thoughts that jump into the mind. People find these thoughts and images disturbing and can't get rid of them. For example, a religious man may have a thought urging him to shout obscenities during a church service, or a caring mother may have intrusive thoughts of causing harm to her baby. Thankfully, people don't carry out these kinds of thoughts, but the obsessions haunt those who have them.

Compulsions are undesired repetitive actions or mental strategies that people with OCD carry out to temporarily reduce anxiety. From time to time, an obsessive thought causes the anxiety; at other times, the anxiety relates to some feared event or situation that triggers the compulsion.

For example, a woman may wash her hands literally hundreds of times each day in order to reduce her anxiety about germs, or a man may have an elaborate nighttime ritual of touching certain objects, lining up clothes in a specific way, arranging his wallet next to his keys in a special position, stacking his change, getting into bed in precisely the correct manner, and reading one section of the Bible before turning out the light. And if he performs any part of the ritual in less than the "perfect" way, he feels compelled to start all over until he gets it right.

Table 1-1 lists common obsessions and compulsions.

Table 1-1   The Most Popular Obsessions
             and Compulsions

Obsessions	Compulsions
Worry about contamination, such as from dirt, germs, radiation, and chemicals.	Excessive hand washing or cleaning due to the obsessive fear of contamination.
Doubts about having remembered to turn the stove off, lock the doors, and so on.	Checking and rechecking to see that the stove is off, doors are locked, and so on.
Perverted sexual imagery that the person feels ashamed of.	Collecting an oversupply of objects that aren't collectibles and have little or no value, such as lint, piles of magazines, string, batteries, and so on.
Unwanted thoughts of harming someone you love.	Repeating rituals over and over again, often with a belief that something bad will happen if the rituals aren't carried out.
Thoughts that would vio-late your own religious beliefs or code in some shameful way.	Arranging items in a rigid, pre-cise way. Often, the person feels compelled to start over if it doesn't come out perfectly.
Thoughts urging you to behave in a socially strange and unacceptable way.	Counting stairs, ceiling tiles, steps walked, and so on ad nauseam.

You may have Obsessive-Compulsive Disorder
(OCD) if you have obsessions, compulsions,
or both. The following are characteristic of
obsessions:

✔ **Your obsessive thoughts don't involve real-life problems.**

For example, if you worry about germs on your hands and you're a brain surgeon, we're glad about that, and you're being realistic. But if you constantly worry about many germs on your hands and you work in a library, you just may have an obsession.

✔ **When the thoughts occur, you try to get rid of them by thinking or doing something else.**

For example, you may have a special prayer or saying that you repeat in your mind over and over again.

✔ **You know that your obsessive thoughts are coming from your own brain and not from some other source.**

In other words, if you think an alien from another planet took over your mind, you have a kind of problem that this book doesn't cover, and you want to get help soon.

✔ **The thoughts bother you considerably.**

The following are characteristic of *compulsions:*

✔ Compulsions are actions and behaviors or mental strategies that you feel compelled to repeat again and again in response to one of your obsessive thoughts or because you have a belief in some rigid rule that you feel can't be broken.

✔ You believe that your compulsive acts can in some way prevent a terrible event from happening or alleviate your anxiety, but what you do doesn't make much sense.

The OCD cycle

A pattern frequently develops in which obsessive thoughts create anxiety, which causes a person to engage in a compulsive act in order to reduce the anxiety and obtain relief. That temporary relief powerfully encourages the person to believe that the compulsive acts help. Unfortunately, because the obsessive thoughts return, the cycle begins again.

Seeing OCD when it's not there

You may recall walking to school with your friends and avoiding cracks in the sidewalk. If you accidentally stepped on one, perhaps someone chided, "If you step on a crack, you'll break your mother's back!" And perhaps sometimes you walked to school by yourself, and that same thought occurred to you, so you avoided stepping on the cracks. Obviously you knew that stepping on a crack wouldn't break your mother's back. So not stepping on cracks almost qualifies as a compulsion. That's because you may have done it repeatedly and known it wouldn't stop anything bad from happening. If you did it simply as a game and it didn't bother you that much, avoiding cracks was no big deal, and it wasn't. Besides, kids often have magical or superstitious thinking, which they usually outgrow.

Avoiding anxiety only worsens anxiety

Avoidance underlies all the anxiety disorders. No one likes to feel anxious. People generally respond to anxiety by steering clear of the things that make them anxious. It makes sense, doesn't it?

Well, yes and no. At the moment of avoidance, anxiety decreases. The problem is that the momentary relief actually increases the desire to continue avoiding the situation. Furthermore, the range of feared events starts to increase. Check out the following example:

Nate doesn't like going to parties, especially weddings. He worries that someone may ask him to dance and that he'll look like a fool on the dance floor. He also worries about making conversations appropriately and not wearing the right thing. At first, he finds it fairly easy to avoid weddings. He simply turns down invitations with one excuse or another and sighs with relief each time he gets out of one.

His sense of relief encourages Nate to start avoiding more social situations, and he declines invitations to other types of parties, family gatherings, and after-work get-togethers. Each act of avoidance briefly soothes his anxiety.

However, Nate finds himself increasingly isolated, and his anxiety starts to show up in almost any situation with people around. Now he feels tense talking at work; he avoids using the telephone when he can, and he stays away from the break room at work. What started as a manageable fear now consumes his life.

That's how avoidance works. Avoidance fertilizes your fears. With enough avoidance, anxiety grows out of control.

Everyone avoids a few things. You may avoid snakes, which is no big deal because they're pretty easy to avoid. You may even avoid an occasional social gathering that makes you anxious. As long as you force yourself to go to at least some social gatherings, your anxiety won't likely blossom.

On the other hand, if some part of you really worried that your mother might suffer if you stepped on a crack, and if you couldn't even get to school because of your worry, you probably had a full-blown compulsion.

Many people check the locks more than once, go back to make sure the coffee pot is turned off a couple of extra times, or count stairs or steps unnecessarily. Only when doing these things starts taking too much time and interferes with relationships, work, or everyday life do you really have a problem.

Lisa's extreme preoccupation with hanging on to objects of no value, which only serve to clutter up her home, is an example of someone with OCD. Lisa is a collector, but you couldn't really call her a collector in the way most people think about collecting because what she accumulates never has any real value to anyone. She keeps every rubber band that holds her daily newspaper together; she never throws away a magazine; and her garage holds nothing but a hodge-podge of batteries, string, pebbles, pieces of wire, nuts and bolts, and scraps of paper. Lisa simply can't get herself to throw anything away. Her house bursts at the seams with useless junk.

But Lisa thinks that just maybe one day she may need a few of these items. When she does think of what she might need, she can rarely find it through all the piles of rubble. As the years go by, Lisa becomes isolated. She can't invite anyone over out of embarrassment for the way her house looks. Lisa's obsession causes her to fret about not having something she needs. Thus, she has a compulsion to never throw anything out. Lisa suffers from OCD.

Chapter 2

Determining Whether You Have an Anxiety Problem

*T*he physical symptoms of anxiety can be a part of normal, everyday experience. But sometimes they signal something more serious. How about you? Have you ever thought you were suffering a nervous breakdown or worried that you were going crazy?

In this chapter, we help you figure out what's going on — whether you're suffering from an anxiety disorder, normal anxiety, or something else. You also get to see how your body responds to anxiety. (Check out Chapter 1 to find out about the major types of anxiety.)

To demonstrate the difference between something as serious as an anxiety disorder and a normal reaction, read the following description and imagine ten minutes in the life of Tiffany.

At first, **Tiffany** feels restless and slightly bored. Standing, she shifts her weight from foot to foot. Walking forward a little, she notices a slight tightening of her chest. Her breathing quickens. She feels an odd mixture of excitement and mounting tension. She sits down and does her best to relax, but the anxiety continues to intensify. Her body suddenly jerks forward; she grips the sides of her seat and clenches her teeth to choke back a scream. Her stomach feels like it might come up through her throat. Then it settles down. She feels her heart race and her face flush. Her stomach seems to push up into her throat again. Tiffany's emotions run wild. Dizziness, fear, and a rushing sensation overtake her. It all comes in waves, one after the other.

You may wonder what's wrong with poor Tiffany. Maybe she has an anxiety disorder. Or possibly she's suffering a nervous breakdown. Perhaps she's going crazy.

But Tiffany spent those ten minutes plus many more at an amusement park. First, she waited in line to buy a ticket and felt bored. Then she handed her ticket to the attendant and buckled herself into a roller coaster. After that, we guess you understand the rest of her experience. Tiffany doesn't have an anxiety disorder, she isn't suffering a nervous breakdown, and she isn't going crazy. As her story illustrates, the symptoms of anxiety can be a normal reaction to life events.

Sorting Out What's Normal from What's Not

Imagine a life with no anxiety at all. How wonderful. You awaken every morning anticipating nothing but pleasant experiences. You fear nothing. The future holds only sweet security and joy.

Think again. With no anxiety, when the guy in the car in front of you slams on the brakes, your response is slower, and you crash. With no worries about the future, your retirement may end up bleak. The total absence of anxiety may cause you to walk into a work presentation unprepared.

Anxiety is good for you! It prepares you to take action. It mobilizes your body for emergencies. It warns you about impending doom. Be glad you have some anxiety. Your anxiety helps you stay out of trouble.

Anxiety only poses a problem for you when

- ✔ Anxiety lasts uncomfortably long or occurs too often.

- ✔ Anxiety interferes with doing what you want to do.

- ✔ Anxiety greatly exceeds the level of actual danger or risk. In other words, when your body and mind feel like an avalanche is about to bury you, but all you have to do is take a test for school, your anxiety has gone too far.

- ✔ You struggle to control your worries, but they disturb you and never let up.

Knowing what anxiety isn't

Symptoms of anxiety may travel with other company. Thus, you may have anxiety along with other emotional disorders. In fact, about half of those with anxiety disorders develop depression, especially if their anxiety goes untreated. (We cover depression in Chapters 5 through 7.) The treatment of other emotional problems differs somewhat from the treatment of anxiety, so knowing the difference between those problems and anxiety is important. Of course, people sometimes have both.

In addition, medications and medical conditions can mimic anxious symptoms. You may think that you're terribly anxious, but actually you may be ill or suffering from the side effects of a drug. See the section "Mimicking Anxiety: Drugs and Diseases," later in this chapter, for details.

Other emotional disorders

Anxiety often accompanies other emotional problems. However, we want you to know that if you have anxiety, it means nothing about whether you have one of the following disorders. So realize that anxiety is not one of the following emotional disorders:

- **Depression:** Depression can feel like life in slow motion. You lose interest in activities that used to bring you pleasure. You feel sad. Most likely, you feel tired, and you sleep fitfully. Your appetite may wane, and your sex drive may droop. Similar to anxiety, you may find it difficult to concentrate or plan ahead. But unlike anxiety, depression saps your drive and motivation. See Chapters 5 through 7 for more information.

- **Bipolar Disorders:** These disorders seesaw between ups and downs. At times, you feel that you're on top of the world. You have grandiose ideas and need little sleep. You may invest in risky schemes, shop recklessly, engage in sexual escapades, or lose your good judgment in other nefarious ways. You may start working frantically on important projects or find ideas streaming through your mind. Then suddenly you crash and burn. Your mood turns sour, and depression sets in.

- **Psychosis:** Psychosis may make you feel anxious, but its symptoms profoundly disrupt life. Psychosis weaves hallucinations into everyday life. For example, some people hear voices talking to them or see shadowy figures when no one is around. Delusions, another feature of psychosis, also distort reality. Common psychotic delusions include believing that the CIA or aliens are tracking your whereabouts. Other delusions involve grandiose beliefs, such as thinking you're Jesus Christ or that you have a special mission to save the world.

If you think that you hear the phone ringing when you're drying your hair or in the shower, only to discover that it wasn't, you're not psychotic. Most people occasionally hear or see trivial things that aren't there. It's only when these perceptions seriously depart from reality that you may worry about psychosis. Fortunately, anxiety disorders don't lead to psychosis.

✔ **Substance abuse:** When people develop a dependency on drugs or alcohol, withdrawal may create serious anxiety. The symptoms of drug or alcohol withdrawal include tremors, disrupted sleep, sweating, increased heartbeat, agitation, and tension. However, if these symptoms only come on in response to a recent cessation of substance use, you don't have an anxiety disorder. On the other hand, people with anxiety disorders sometimes abuse substances in a misguided attempt to control their anxiety.

Mimicking Anxiety: Drugs and Diseases

As common as anxiety disorders are, believing that you're suffering from anxiety when you're not is all too easy. Prescription drugs may have a variety of side effects, some of which mimic some of the symptoms of anxiety. Various medical conditions also produce symptoms that imitate the signs of anxiety.

Exploring anxiety-mimicking drugs

The pharmaceutical industry reports on the most widely prescribed categories of medications every year. To show you how easily medication side effects can resemble the symptoms of anxiety, we list the top ten of the most widely prescribed drugs and their anxiety-mimicking side effects in Table 2-1. These medications have many other side effects that we don't list here.

Table 2-1		Angst in the Medicine Cabinet	
Popularity	*Drug Name*	*Purpose*	*Anxiety-like Side Effects*
No. 1	Codeine	Alleviate pain and manage nonproductive cough	Agitation, dizziness, nausea, decreased appetite, palpitations, flushing, and restlessness
No. 2	Calcium channel blockers	Stabilize angina and reduce high blood pressure	Dizziness, flushing, palpitations, diarrhea, gastric upset, insomnia, anxiety, confusion, light-headedness, and fatigue
No. 3	Anti-ulcerants	Treatment of ulcers	Dizziness, anxiety, confusion, headache, weakness, diarrhea, flushing, sweating, and tremors

Popularity	Drug Name	Purpose	Anxiety-like Side Effects
No. 4	Angiotensin-converting enzyme (ACE) inhibitors	Reduce high blood pressure	Impotence, dizziness, insomnia, headaches, nausea, vomiting, and weakness
No. 5	Selective serotonin reuptake inhibitors (SSRIs)	Treatment of depression, anxiety, and bulimia	Headache, insomnia, anxiety, tremors, dizziness, nervousness, fatigue, poor concentration, agitation, nausea, diarrhea, decreased appetite, sweating, hot flashes, palpitations, twitching, and impotence
No. 6	Statins	Cholesterol reduction	Headache, dizziness, diarrhea, nausea, muscle cramps, and tremors
No. 7	Beta blockers	Reduce angina & high blood pressure, treat dysrhythmias	Dizziness, diarrhea, nausea, palpitations, impotence, and disorientation

(continued)

Table 2-1 *(continued)*

Popularity	Drug Name	Purpose	Anxiety-like Side Effects
No. 8	Hormone replacement medications	Reduce menopause symptoms, treat osteoporosis, and treat ovarian failure	Dizziness, headache, nausea, vomiting, diarrhea, and appetite changes
No. 9	Anti-arthritic and anti-inflammatory medications	Treat arthritis and pain	Fatigue, anxiety, dizziness, nervousness, insomnia, nausea, vomiting, sweating, tremors, confusion, and shortness of breath
No. 10	Benzodiazepines	Treat anxiety	Dizziness, headhache, anxiety, tremors, stimulation, insomnia, nausea, and diarrhea

Interesting isn't it? Even medications for the treatment of anxiety can produce anxiety-like side effects. Of course, most people don't experience such side effects with these medications, but they do occur. If you're taking one or more of the preceding commonly prescribed drugs and feel anxious, you may want to check with your doctor.

In addition, various over-the-counter medications may have anxiety-mimicking side effects. These medications include cold remedies, bronchodilators, and decongestants. Also, many types of aspirin contain caffeine, which can produce symptoms of anxiety if consumed excessively. These medications can cause restlessness, heart palpitations, tension, shortness of breath, and irritability.

Angst from over the counter

One of the most common ingredients in over-the-counter cold medications is *pseudoephedrine,* a popular and effective decongestant. I, Charles Elliott (one of the two-author team that's writing this book), specialize in the treatment of panic and anxiety disorders. A couple of years ago, I had a bad cold and cough for longer than usual. I treated it with the strongest over-the-counter medications that I could find. Not only that, I took a little more than the label called for during the day so I could see clients without coughing through the session. One day during that period, I noticed an unusually rapid heartbeat and considerable tightness in breathing. I wondered for a while if I was having a panic attack. It didn't seem possible, but the symptoms stared me in the face. Could I possibly have caught a Panic Disorder from my clients?

Not exactly. Upon reflection, I realized that perhaps I'd taken more than just a little too much of the cold medication containing pseudoephedrine. I stopped taking the medication, and the symptoms disappeared, never to return.

So be careful with over-the-counter medications. Read the directions carefully. Don't try to be your own doctor like I did!

Investigating medical anxiety imposters

More than a few types of diseases and medical conditions can create anxiety-like symptoms, too. That's why we strongly recommend, especially if you're experiencing significant anxiety for the first time, that you visit your doctor. Your doctor can help you sort out whether you have a physical problem, a reaction to a medication, an emotionally based anxiety problem, or some combination of these.

Table 2-2 lists some of the medical conditions that produce symptoms of anxiety. In addition, merely getting sick can cause anxiety about your illness. For example, if you receive a serious diagnosis of heart disease, certain cancers, or a chronic progressive disorder, you are likely to develop some anxiety about dealing with the consequences of what you've been told.

Table 2-2	Medical Imposters	
Medical Condition	*What It Is*	*Anxiety-like Symptoms*
Hypoglycemia	Low blood sugar, sometimes associated with other disorders or can occur by itself. It is a common complication of diabetes.	Confusion, irritability, trembling, sweating, rapid heartbeat, weakness, and a cold, clammy feeling.
Hyperthyroidism	Excess amount of thyroid hormone. It has various causes.	Nervousness, restlessness, sweating, fatigue, sleep disturbance, nausea, tremors, and diarrhea.

Medical Condition	*What It Is*	*Anxiety-like Symptoms*
Other hormonal imbalances	Various conditions associated with fluctuations in hormone levels, such as premenstrual syndrome (PMS), menopause, or postpartum. Highly variable symptoms.	Tension, irritability, headaches, mood swings, compulsive behavior, fatigue, and panic.
Lupus	An autoimmune disease in which the patient's immune system attacks certain types of its own cells.	Anxiety, poor concentration, irritability, headaches, irregular heartbeat, and impaired memory.
Mitral valve prolapse	The mitral valve of the heart fails to close properly, allowing blood to flow back into the left atrium. Often confused with panic attacks in making the diagnosis.	Palpitations, shortness of breath, fatigue, chest pain, and difficulty breathing.
Ménière's syndrome	An inner ear disorder that includes vertigo, loss of hearing, and ringing or other noises in the ear.	Vertigo that includes abnormal sensations associated with movement, dizziness, nausea, vomiting, and sweating.

The chicken or the egg:
Irritable bowel syndrome

Irritable bowel syndrome (IBS) is a common condition that involves a variety of related problems, usually including cramps or pain in the abdomen, diarrhea, and/or constipation. These problems occur in people with no known physical problems in their digestive systems. For many years, doctors told most of their patients that irritable bowel syndrome (IBS) was caused exclusively by stress, worry, and anxiety.

In 1999, Catherine Woodman, MD, and colleagues discovered a mutated gene in patients with irritable bowel syndrome more often than in those without it. Interestingly, that same rogue gene also occurs more often in those with Panic Disorders (see Chapter 1 for more about these disorders). Other possible physical causes of IBS may have to do with poor communication between muscles and nerves in the colon.

Various medications have been found to decrease some of the worst symptoms of IBS. In addition, psychotherapy that teaches relaxation techniques, biofeedback, and techniques for coping with anxiety and stress also improves IBS symptoms. So at this point, no one really knows how much of IBS is due to physical causes, anxiety, or stress. More likely, however, the mind and body interact in important ways that can't always be separated.

Preparing to Fight or Run

Your body responds to threats by preparing for action in three different ways: physically, mentally, and behaviorally. When danger presents itself, you reflexively prepare to stand and fight or run like you've never run before. Your body mobilizes for peril in complex and fantastic ways. Figure 2-1 gives you the picture.

First, your brain sends signals through your nervous system to go on high alert. It tells the adrenal glands to rev up production of adrenalin and noradrenalin. These hormones stimulate the body in various ways. Your heart pounds faster, and you start breathing more rapidly, sending increased oxygen to your lungs, while blood flows to the large muscles, preparing them to fight or flee from danger.

Digestion slows to preserve energy for meeting the challenge, and pupils dilate to improve vision. Blood flow decreases to hands and feet in order to prevent blood loss if injury occurs and to keep up the blood supply to the large muscles. Sweating increases in order to keep the body cool, and it makes you slippery so aggressors can't grab hold of you. All your muscles tense to spring into action.

Mentally, you automatically scan your surroundings intensely. Your attention focuses on the threat and nothing else. In fact, you can't attend to much of anything else.

Behaviorally, you're now ready to run or fight. You need that preparation in the face of danger. When you have to take on a bear, a lion, or a warrior, you'd better have all your resources on high alert.

Just one problem — in today's world, most people don't encounter lions and bears. Unfortunately, your body reacts too easily with the same preparation to fight traffic, meet deadlines, speak in public, and other everyday worries.

When human beings have nothing to fight or run from, all that energy has to get out somehow. So you may feel the urge to fidget by moving your feet and hands. You feel like jumping out of your skin. You may impulsively rant or rave with those around you.

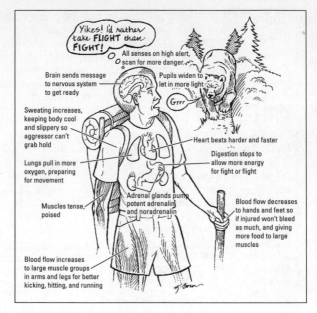

Figure 2-1: Choices, choices!

Most experts believe that if you experience the physical effects of anxiety on a frequent, chronic basis, it can't be doing you any good. Various studies have suggested the possibility that chronic anxiety and stress could conceivably contribute to a variety of physical problems, such as abnormal heart rhythms, high blood pressure, irritable bowel syndrome, asthma, ulcers, stomach upset, acid reflux, chronic muscle spasms, tremors, chronic back pain, tension headaches, and a depressed immune system. Figure 2-2 illustrates the toll of chronic anxiety on the body.

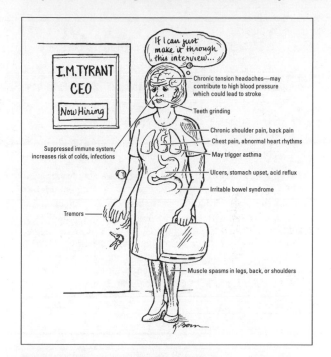

Figure 2-2: The chronic effects of anxiety.

However, before you get too anxious about your anxiety, please realize that hard, definitive evidence doesn't exist yet that shows that anxiety is a major cause of most of these problems. Nevertheless, enough studies have suggested that it can make these disorders worse and that you should probably take chronic anxiety seriously. In other words, have concern, but not panic.

Defending against diabetes

If just the misery of chronic anxiety isn't enough, here are a couple more reasons to work on getting rid of excess stress:

✔ People with long-lasting stress are significantly more likely to develop type 2 diabetes.

✔ This isn't surprising, because stress increases the levels of glucose in the bloodstream.

Researchers at Duke University conducted a study with over 100 subjects and found that when stress management was added to the care of adults with diabetes, their blood sugar actually went down. These techniques weren't complex or time consuming. The amazing result of this study was that the glucose levels of those who found out how to calm down dropped as much as you would expect had the subjects been taking an extra diabetes-control drug. So if you don't have diabetes, protect yourself by overcoming anxiety, and if you do have diabetes, calm thoughts may help you and your doctor control the disease.

Chapter 3

Making Changes to Overcome Anxiety

*T*he odds are that if you're reading this book, you want to do something about your own anxiety or help someone you love. If so, you should know that people start on the path to change with the best intentions, but as they move along, suddenly they encounter icy conditions and lose traction, spin their wheels, and slide off the road.

This chapter gives you ways to throw salt and sand on the ice and keep moving. First, we explain where anxiety comes from. When you understand the origins of anxiety, you can move from self-blame to self-acceptance, thus allowing yourself to direct your energy away from self-abuse and toward more productive activities. Next, we show you the other big barriers that tend to block the way to change. Finally, we give you effective strategies to keep you safely on the road to overcoming anxiety.

Digging Out the Roots of Anxiety

The three major causes of anxiety are

- ✔ **Genetics:** Your biological inheritance
- ✔ **Parenting:** The way that you were reared
- ✔ **Trauma:** The vexing events of everyday life

Studies show that when people experience an unanticipated trauma, only a minority ends up with severe anxiety because anxiety usually stems from a combination of causes — perhaps genes and trauma or trauma and parenting, or sometimes all three gang up to induce anxiety. At the same time, just one factor, if formidable enough, could possibly cause the entire problem.

For example, **Bonnie** manages to grow up in a drug war zone without developing terribly distressing symptoms. Bullets whiz through her bedroom window one night, and one pierces her abdomen. She shows surprising resilience during her recovery. Surely, she must have some robust, anti-anxiety genes and perhaps some pretty good parents as well in order to successfully endure such an experience. However, when she is raped at the age of 16, she develops serious problems with anxiety — she has sustained one trauma too many.

Thus, you can never ascertain the exact cause of anyone's anxiety with absolute certainty. However, if you examine someone's childhood relationship with his or her parents, family history, and the various events in one's life (such as accidents, war, disease, and so on), you can generally come up with some pretty good ideas as to why anxiety now causes problems. If you have anxiety, consider reviewing these fomenters of distress and think about which ones may have caused you the most trouble.

But what difference does it make where your anxiety comes from? Overcoming anxiety doesn't absolutely require knowledge of where it originated. The remedies change little whether you were born with anxiety or acquired it much later in your life.

Identifying the source of your anxiety can help you to realize that your anxiety isn't something that you brought on yourself. Anxiety develops for a number of good, solid reasons. The blame doesn't belong with the person who has anxiety.

Guilt and self-blame can only sap your energy. They drain your resources and keep your focus away from the effort required for challenging your anxiety. By contrast, self-forgiveness and self-acceptance invigorate and vitalize your efforts.

Sleuthing your genetic villains

If you suffer from excessive worries and tension, look around at the rest of your family. Of those who have an anxiety disorder, typically about a quarter of their relatives suffer along with them. So your Uncle Ralph may not struggle with anxiety, but Aunt Melinda or your sister Charlene just may.

Genetic goofs

Studies have shown a genetic mutation in people with anxiety disorders that affects the availability of the brain's neurotransmitter *serotonin,* which is believed to contribute to emotional well-being. If you don't have enough serotonin floating around in your brain, you're likely to fall prey to worries, anxiety, or the blues. Medications can increase the availability of serotonin in the brain.

But if Uncle Ralph, Aunt Melinda, and your sister Charlene all suffer from anxiety and all had to live with Grandma, you may argue that Grandma would make anyone anxious. In other words, they all lived in an anxiety-inducing environment. Maybe their anxiety has nothing to do with their genes.

Various researchers have studied siblings and twins who live together to verify that genes do play an important role in how people experience and cope with anxiety. As predicted, identical twins were far more similar to each other in terms of anxiety than fraternal twins or other siblings. But even if you're born with a genetic predisposition toward anxiety, other factors such as your environment, peers, and how your parents raised you enter into the mix.

It's my parents' fault!

Parent bashing is in. Blaming parents for almost anything that ails you is easy. Parents usually do the best they can. Raising children poses a formidable task, so in most cases, parents don't deserve to be vilified. However, they do hold responsibility for the way that you were brought up and thus may have contributed to your woes.

Three parenting styles appear to foster anxiety in children:

- **Overprotective:** These parents shield their kids from every imaginable stress or harm. If their kids stumble, they swoop them up before they even hit the ground. When their kids get upset, they fix the problem. Not surprisingly, their kids fail to find out how to tolerate fear, anxiety, or frustration.

- **Over-controlling:** These parents micro-manage all their children's activities. They direct every detail, from how their children should play to what they should wear to how they solve arithmetic problems. They discourage independence and fertilize dependency and anxiety.

✔ **Inconsistent:** The parents in this group provide their kids with erratic rules and limits. One day, they respond with understanding when their kids have trouble with their homework; the next day, they explode when their kids ask for help. These kids fail to discover the connection between their own efforts and a predictable outcome. Therefore, they feel that they have little control over what happens in life. It's no wonder that they feel anxious.

It's the world's fault!

The world today moves at a faster pace than ever, and the work week has gradually inched upward rather than the other way around. Modern life is rife with both complexity and danger. Perhaps that's why mental health workers see more people with anxiety-related problems than ever before. Four specific types of vexing events can trigger a problem with anxiety, even in someone who has never suffered from it much before:

✔ **Unanticipated threats:** Predictability and stability counteract anxiety, and the opposite fuels it. For example, **Calvin** works long hours to make a decent living. Nevertheless, he lives from paycheck to paycheck with little left for savings. A freak slip on an icy patch of sidewalk disables him for six weeks, and he has insufficient sick leave to cover his absence. He now worries obsessively over his ability to pay bills. Even when he returns to work, he worries more than ever about the next financial booby trap that awaits him.

✔ **Escalating demands:** Nothing is better than a pro-motion. At least that's what **Jake** thinks when his supervisor hands him a once-in-a-lifetime oppor-tunity to direct the new high-risk Research & Development division at work. Jake never expected such a lofty position this early in his career or the doubling of his salary. Of course, new duties, expectations, and responsibilities come along for the ride. Jake now begins to fret and worry. What if he fails to meet the challenge? Anxiety starts taking over his life.

✔ **Confidence killers: Tricia** is on top of the world. She has a good job and feels ecstatic about her upcoming wedding. However, she is stunned when her fiancé backs out of the proposal. Now she worries incessantly that something is wrong with her; perhaps she'll never have the life she envisioned for herself.

✔ **Terrorizing trauma:** No one ever wants to experience a horrifying or even life-threatening experience. Unfortunately, these bitter pills do happen. Sexual abuse, horrific accidents, battlefield injuries, and rape have occurred for centuries, and we suspect that they always will. When they do, severe problems with anxiety often emerge. (See Chapter 1 for information about Post-Traumatic Stress Disorder.)

Moving from Self-Abuse to Self-Acceptance

Time and again, we see our worried, tense clients suffer from another needless source of pain: self-abuse. Their anxiety is bad enough, but they also pound on themselves *because* they have anxiety.

If you do this to yourself, we suggest that you try Gary's approach to self-forgiveness.

Gary developed a Panic Disorder. His attacks of feeling nauseous, dizzy, out of breath, and thinking he's going crazy have increased recently. He feels deep shame and embarrassment that someone like him has this problem. When he starts having panic attacks at work, he finally caves in and seeks help. He tells his psychologist that a real man would never have this kind of problem. His psychologist helps Gary to be more self-forgiving. He asks Gary to write down the three major causes of his anxiety. He tells him to thoroughly review his life and come up with as many possible contributors to his worries as he can. Look at Table 3-1 to see what Gary came up with.

Table 3-1	Gary's Anxiety Causes	
Possible Genetic Influence	*Parenting*	*Events: Old and New*
My Aunt Mary hardly ever leaves her house. Maybe she has something like I do.	Well, my father had quite an unpredictable temper. I never knew when he'd blow.	When I was 6 years old, we had a terrible car accident, and I spent three days in the hospital. I was scared.
My mother is high strung.	My mother's moods bounced all over the place. I could never tell how she'd react when I asked her for something.	My middle school was in a terrible neighborhood. Gangs ruled. I had to look over my shoulder at every turn.

(continued)

Table 3-1 *(continued)*

Possible Genetic Influence Parenting	Events: Old and New
My cousin Margarite seems shy. Maybe she has too much anxiety.	My first marriage ended when I caught my wife cheating. I couldn't believe she'd do something like that. Even though I trust my new wife, I worry too much about her faithfulness.
My brother worries all the time. He seems totally stressed.	Two years ago, I was diagnosed with diabetes. I worry too much about my health now.

If you'd like to better understand the causes of your anxiety, write them down like Gary did in Table 3-1. Separate your paper into columns topped with the same headings: "Possible Genetic Influence," "Parenting," and "Events: Old and New." Take your time; don't rush it. You may write several drafts before you come up with a definitive list. You may want to do this task over several days.

After you list the likely culprits that led to your distress, ask yourself some questions like the ones that follow:

✔ Did I ask for my anxiety?

✔ Was there ever a time in my life that I actually wanted to feel anxious?

✔ Am I primarily to blame for my worries?

✔ What percentage of the blame can I realistically assign to myself as opposed to genes, parenting, and events, both old and new?

✔ If a couple of friends of mine had troubles with anxiety, what would I say to them? Would I think they were to blame? Would I think as ill of them as I do myself?

✔ Does thinking badly about myself help me to get over my anxiety?

✔ If I decided to stop pummeling myself, would I have more energy for tackling my problems?

Hopefully, answering the preceding questions can help you move toward self-acceptance. When you discover that having anxiety means nothing about your worth or value as a human being, you just might lighten up on yourself a little. We recommend it highly. If you find yourself completely unable to let go of self-abuse, you may want to seek professional help. Mind you, people get down on themselves at times, but chronic, unrelenting self-abuse is another matter.

Having Second Thoughts about Change

Clearly, no one likes feeling anxious, tense, and nervous, and anxiety may climb to such heights that it overwhelms personal resources and the capacity to cope. Chronic, severe anxiety frequently serves as a prelude to serious depression. Obviously, anyone experiencing this torment would jump at the chance to do something about it.

With good intentions, people buy self-help books, attend workshops, and even seek therapy. They fully intend to make meaningful changes in their lives. However, as the old proverb puts it, "Hell is paved with good intentions."

Have you ever gone to a health club in January? The clubs are packed with new, enthusiastic members. By mid-March, health clubs return to normal. Like so many New Year's resolutions, the initial burst of resolve too often fades. What happens to all that determination?

When you bought this book, you may have vowed to do something about your anxiety once and for all. Like the January health club enthusiasts, you may still feel motivated and focused. If so, feel free to skip this section.

If you start losing your willpower or your belief in your ability to do something about your anxiety, come back to this section! It can help you get back on track.

What happens to the folks at the health clubs in March? Usually, they think they've simply lost their willpower. Actually, interfering thoughts creep into their minds and steal away their motivation. They start to think that they don't have the time or the money or that they can get in shape later. Such thoughts seduce them into abandoning their goals.

Thoughts about abandoning your quest to overcome anxiety may disrupt your efforts at some point. If so, the first step involves identifying which thoughts stream through your mind. In the following section, we give you strategies for fighting them off. So now, here are our top ten excuses for staying stuck:

10. Anxiety isn't really that big of a problem for me. I thought it was when I bought this book, but my

anxiety isn't as bad as some of the people I've been reading about. Maybe it's not that big of a deal.

9. If I try and fail, I'll make a fool out of myself. My friends and family would think I was stupid to even try.

8. My anxiety feels too overwhelming to tackle. I just don't know if I could handle the additional stress of even thinking about it.

7. I'm afraid of trying and not getting anywhere. That would make me feel even worse than if I did nothing at all. I'd feel like a failure.

6. Feelings can't really be controlled. It's just fooling yourself to think otherwise. You feel the way you feel.

5. I'll do something about my anxiety when I feel the motivation. Right now, I don't really feel like it. I'm sure the motivation will come; I just have to wait for it.

4. Who would I be without my anxiety? That's just who I am. I'm an anxious person; it's just me.

3. I don't believe I can really change. After all, I've been this way my entire life. Books like these don't work anyway.

2. I'm too busy to do anything about my anxiety. These activities look like they take time. I could never work it into my hectic schedule.

1. The number one reason people stay stuck: I'm too anxious to do anything about my anxiety. Whenever I think about confronting my anxiety, it makes me feel worse.

Look over our preceding list several times. Mull over each excuse and circle any that seem familiar or reasonable to you. Any excuses that you agree with will hinder your progress. Now we have some ways for you to challenge these excuses, no matter how reasonable they may seem.

Deciding if You Really Want to Get the Show on the Road

If any of our top ten excuses for staying stuck resonate with you, then your decision to overcome anxiety is not stable. Those thoughts can sabotage your best intentions. Don't underestimate their power.

We have three types of strategies for helping you turn your intentions into actions:

- ✔ **Debate the decision with yourself.**

  List your excuses for staying stuck and match them with reasons to move ahead.

- ✔ **Don't wait for a magical motivating moment.**
- ✔ **Kick-start your program.**

Half-hearted decisions lead to procrastination and avoidance of the task at hand. Anxiety hurts, but change is hard. The next section shows you how to push aside your fear of change.

Debating the decision

Pretend that you're judging a debate. One side favors the status quo, in other words, not changing. The other side takes the pro-change position. Ask which side makes the most sense; then declare a victor.

Miguel worries about everything. He wakes up early in the morning with thoughts about what he must do that day for school. He dreams about going to class without his homework and being embarrassed by his teacher. He puts off applying for college out of fear that he won't get in, even though his grades and test scores pose no problem. He feels nervous, tense, and irritable much of the time. Lately, his worries disrupt his concentration to the extent that he spaces out during class lectures. His parents insist that he see a counselor for help with his anxiety, but Miguel doesn't believe it will help. The counselor, making up a chart like Table 3-2, works with him to debate his reluctance to work on overcoming his anxiety.

Table 3-2	Miguel's Great Debate
Excuses for Staying Stuck	*Reasons for Moving Forward*
If I try and fail, I'll make a fool out of myself. My friends and family would think I was stupid to even try.	Many of my friends have seen counselors, and I've never thought poorly of them, even if one or two of them didn't seem to get much better. At least they tried. Besides, I have a pretty good chance of succeeding; I usually do on most things I work at.
I'm afraid of trying and not getting anywhere. That would make me feel even worse than if I did nothing at all. I'd feel like a failure.	The only real failure would be to not do anything at all. This anxiety keeps me from doing the best I in school. I run a bigger risk of failing in school if I stay stuck.
Feelings can't really be controlled. It's just fooling yourself to think otherwise. You feel the way you feel.	Just because I feel it's hopeless to do anything doesn't mean it's true. Many people go to therapy for some reason; surely it makes them feel better, or the world wouldn't have a zillion therapists.
Who would I be without my anxiety? That's just who I am. I'm an anxious person; it's just me.	Anxiety doesn't define who I am. It just gets in my way. I have many fine qualities that won't change.

Which side wins the debate? We think the reasons for moving forward deserve a clear victory.

If you have some excuses for staying stuck, try subjecting them to debate like Miguel did in Table 3-2. List your "Excuses for Staying Stuck" on the left side of a blank sheet of paper and your "Reasons for Moving Forward" on the right. The following questions may help you with developing your arguments for moving forward:

- ✔ Does my excuse catastrophize? In other words, am I exaggerating the truth?

- ✔ Can I find any evidence that would contradict my excuse?

- ✔ Can I think of people to whom my excuse doesn't apply? And if it doesn't apply to them, why should it to me?

- ✔ Am I trying to predict the future with negative thinking when no one can ever know the future?

Taking off from the starting blocks

Some excuses for staying stuck sap your motivation and will to change. One of our top ten excuses for staying stuck hits this issue head on, specifically number five: "I'll do something about my anxiety when I feel the motivation. Right now, I don't really feel like it. I'm sure the motivation will come; I just have to wait for it."

This excuse is based on a common but pernicious misconception. Most people think that they need to wait until motivation hits them before acting. Unfortunately, if you operate on that assumption, you could be in for a long wait, because facing your fears doesn't particularly feel good. It can even increase your anxiety for a little while. You may never *feel* like tackling it. However, if you start to take action and feel a little progress, your motivation surges.

Ellen can't face driving on freeways. She spends an extra hour each day getting to work and back because she takes the side roads. She really can't afford the time or the extra gas and wear on her car.

Ellen decides to get over her fear once and for all. However, each day when she gets in her car, the very thought of trying to drive even a little on the freeway makes her anxious, and she loses her resolve. So she rationalizes that she'll do something about her problem when the commute gets so bad that she feels sufficient motivation to deal with her fear.

Many months pass, the commute remains the same, and so does Ellen's fear of driving on freeways. She realizes that she may never *want* to confront her phobia. So she decides to force herself to drive on the freeway for just a short distance, whether she feels like it or not. Ellen decides to drive a half-mile stretch of the freeway near her home on a Sunday. After she gets home, she is surprised to find herself feeling proud of her small accomplishment and actually wants to do more. Each step she takes increases her motivation.

 Action generally precedes motivation; if you wait to feel like overcoming your anxiety, you may wait a lifetime.

If you find that the idea of dealing with your anxiety is just too much to handle, you may be struggling with the number eight excuse for staying stuck: "My anxiety feels too overwhelming to tackle. I just don't know if I could handle the additional stress of even thinking about it." If so, putting one foot in front of the other may help; take baby steps.

Stop dwelling on the entire task. For example, if you think about all the steps that you'll take over the next five years, that's an incredible amount of walking to ponder. Hundreds if not thousands of miles await you. The mere thought of all those miles could stress you out.

You may, like many folks, wake up early in the morning on some days with a huge list of tasks that you need to do in the coming week. Ugh. A sense of defeat sets in, and you feel like staying in bed for the rest of the day. Dread replaces enthusiasm. If, instead, you clear your mind of the entire agenda and concentrate on only the first item on the list, your distress is likely to diminish, at least a little.

Paula, for example, is about to put this strategy into play. Paula has a Social Phobia (see Chapter 1 for details on Social Phobias). She can't stand the idea of attending social functions. She feels that the moment she walks into a group, all eyes focus on her, which sends her anxiety through the roof. She desperately wants to change. But the idea of attending large parties or company functions overwhelms her with terror. Look at Table 3-3 to see how Paula broke the task down into baby steps.

Table 3-3	Paula's Baby Steps to Success
Goals	*Step-by-Step Breakdown of Actions*
Ultimate goal	Going to a large party, staying the entire time, and talking with numerous people without fear.
Intermediate goal	Attending a small party, staying a little while, and talking to a couple of people, although feeling a little scared.
Small goal	Going to a work-related social hour, staying 30 minutes, and talking to at least one other person in spite of some anxiety.
First baby step	Calling a friend and asking her to go to lunch in spite of anxiety.

This simple strategy works because the overwhelming task is broken down into manageable pieces. Sit down and chart out your ultimate goal. Then chart a goal that isn't quite so lofty that could serve as a stepping stone — an intermediate goal. Then chart out the action that would be required of you to meet a small goal. If your intermediate goal feels doable, you can start with it. If not, break it down further. It doesn't matter how small you make your first step. Anything that moves you just a little in the right direction can get you going and increase your confidence with one step at a time.

Maybe you suffer from anxiety, but when it comes to doing something about it, you start thinking that yours isn't all that bad after all. If so, you may be *rationalizing* and letting excuse number ten get in the way: "Anxiety isn't really that big of a problem for me. I thought it was when I bought this book, but my anxiety isn't as bad as some of the people that I've been reading about. Maybe it's not that big of a deal."

On the other hand, perhaps your anxiety doesn't warrant doing anything about it. If so, then that's wonderful! Give this book to a friend who needs it more than you! But how can you figure out if you're in denial or not? Pondering the pros and cons of conquering your anxiety can help you.

Ed directs the accounting department of a large manufacturing plant. He has huge responsibilities, multiple deadlines, and difficult people to supervise. He depends on many people to submit figures for his quarterly report, but sometimes they fail to deliver on time, and Ed needs to confront them. Unfortunately, Ed dreads conflict and avoids speaking. The stress of waiting makes Ed feel nauseous, tense, and irritable. He knows that he has anxiety, but he figures that he's gotten by so far, so he questions whether it's worth trying to change.

Persevering through the peaks and valleys

A group of psychologists conducted extensive research on how people make important changes, such as quitting smoking, losing weight, and overcoming emotional difficulties. They found that change isn't a straightforward process. It includes a number of stages:

- ✔ **Precontemplation:** In this stage, people haven't even given a thought to doing anything about their problem. They may deny having any difficulty at all. If you're reading this book, you're probably not in this stage.

- ✔ **Contemplation:** People start thinking about tackling their problem. But in this stage, it feels a little out of their reach to do anything about it.

- ✔ **Preparation:** In preparation, people develop a plan for change. They gather their resources and make resolutions.

- ✔ **Action:** The real work begins, and the plan goes into action.

- ✔ **Maintenance:** Now is the time to hold one's ground. People must hang tough to prevent sliding back.

- ✔ **Termination:** The change has become habit, so much so that relapse is less likely and further work isn't particularly necessary.

The preceding stages look like a straight line from precontemplation to termination, but what these psychologists found is that people bounce around the stages in various ways. They may go from contemplation to action without having made adequate preparation. Others may reach the maintenance stage and give up on their efforts, slipping back to the precontemplation stage.

Many successful changers bounce back and forth between stages a number of times before finally achieving their goals. So don't get discouraged if that happens to you. Keep your goal in mind and reinitiate your efforts if you slip. Yep. Try, try, and try again.

Ed ponders the pros and cons of tackling his problem. Putting his concerns in perspective, he organizes his thoughts for taking action versus his fears on paper. (Look at Table 3-4 to see how Ed mapped out his pros and cons.) Ed starts by listing the cons of taking action because he's more fully aware of what those are.

Table 3-4   Ed's Cons and Pros for Taking Action

Cons of Taking Action	Pros of Taking Action
It will make me more anxious to confront people.	I suffer from anxiety anyway and worry that I'll get in trouble if I can't get these people to produce on time. If I confront the people that I need to, I'll get more help.
People may not like me if I confront them.	I avoid people so much that they don't even know who I am. So what if a few people don't like me? Feeling less worried about people liking me sounds pretty good.
I'm not terribly unhappy at my job most of the time. My quarterly report just happens once a quarter.	Yes, it only happens once a quarter, but I dread the quarterly report for weeks in advance. Getting rid of the dread sounds worth doing.

When Ed considers his cons and pros carefully, he makes the decision to do something about his discomfort. You can use Ed's chart in Table 3-4 as a sample means of charting out your reasons for and against taking action. If your motivation wanes because you're not sure how serious your problem is, take the time to reflect thoroughly. Generate as many reasons as you can.

Chapter 4

Watching Anxiety Come and Go

● ●

In This Chapter

▶ Tracking your anxiety to gain control

▶ Seeing the bright side

● ●

Anxiety may feel like it will never go away. Believing that you have no control over it and that stress invades your every waking moment is easy. This chapter helps you to realize that anxiety actually has an ebb and flow. Then we show you how taking a few minutes to write down your feelings each day may discharge a little of your anxiety and possibly improve your health. Finally, we help you understand that progress, like anxiety, ebbs and flows.

Following Your Fears All the Way Down the Line

One of the best early steps that you can take to conquer anxiety is to simply follow it every day in a couple of different ways. Why would you want to do all that? After all, you already know full well that you're anxious.

Watching your worries starts the process of change. You discover important patterns, triggers, and insights into your anxiety.

Observing your anxiety from stem to stern

Observing anxiety fulfills several useful functions:

- ✔ First, monitoring forces you to be aware of your emotions. Avoiding and running away from troubling emotions only causes them to escalate.

- ✔ Second, you see that your anxiety goes up and down throughout the day — not quite as upsetting as thinking it rules every moment of your life. You're also likely to discover that recording your ratings can help you to take charge and feel more in control of what's going on inside of you.

- ✔ Finally, keeping track helps you to see how you're progressing in your efforts to quell your distress. Virginia's story shows you how.

Virginia complains to her friends that she's the most nervous person on the planet and that she's close to a nervous breakdown. Recently, her father had heart surgery and her husband lost his job. Virginia feels completely out of control and says that her anxiety never stops. When her counselor suggests that she start tracking her anxiety, she tells him, "You've got to be kidding. I don't need to do that. I can tell you right now that I'm anxious all the time. There's no let up." He urges her to go ahead and try anyway.

Table 4-1 shows what Virginia comes up with in her first week of tracking. On a scale of one to ten — ten being total panic and one being complete calm — Virginia rates the level of anxiety that she experiences at around the same time in the morning, then again in the afternoon, and later in the evening.

Table 4-1   Virginia's Day-by-Day Anxiety Levels

Day	Morning	Afternoon	Evening	Daily Average
Sunday	4	6	8	**6**
Monday	6	7	9	**7.3**
Tuesday	5	6	6	**5.7**
Wednesday	4	5	7	**5.3**
Thursday	3	8	8	**6.3**
Friday	5	9	9	**7.7**
Saturday	3	5	5	**4.3**
Average	**4.3**	**6.6**	**7.4**	**6.1**

Virginia discovers a few things. First, she notices that her anxiety is routinely less intense in the morning. It also tends to escalate in the afternoon and peak in the evenings. With only one week's records, she can't discern if her anxiety level is decreasing, increasing, or remaining stable. However, she notices feeling a little better simply because she feels like she's starting to take charge of her problem. She also realizes that some days are better than others and that her anxiety varies instead of overwhelming her all the time.

 Track your anxiety in a notebook for a few weeks. Carry your anxiety-tracking notebook with you and try to fill it out at the same times each day. Notice patterns or differences in intensity.

Writing about your worries, warts and all

Millions of people keep a diary at some point in their lives. Some develop daily writing as a lifelong habit. Logically, people who keep journals must feel that they get something out of their writing or they wouldn't do it. Keeping a journal of life's emotionally significant events has surprising benefits:

- ✔ Journal writing appears to decrease the number of visits people make to the doctor for physical complaints.

- ✔ It increases the production of T cells, which are beneficial to the immune system.

- ✔ Keeping a journal about emotional events improved the grades of a group of college students as compared to those students who wrote about trivial matters.

- ✔ Recently, unemployed workers who wrote about the trauma of losing their jobs found new employment more quickly than those who didn't.

Journal writing doesn't have rules. You can write about anything, anywhere and anytime. However, if you want the full benefits of writing in a journal, we encourage you to write about feelings and the emotionally important events of your life. Write about anything that troubles you during the day and/or your past difficulties. Spend a little time on it.

Writing about past traumas may bring you considerable relief. However, if you find that the task floods you with overwhelming grief or anxiety, you'll probably find it helpful to seek professional assistance.

Writing about your distressing feelings makes a great start. However, if you'd like more bang for your buck, take a few extra minutes and write about what you feel grateful for each day. Why? Positive emotions help counteract negative emotions. Writing about your boons and blessings improves mood, increases optimism, and may benefit your health.

At first blush, you may think that you have little to be grateful for. Anxiety can so easily cloud vision. Did your mother ever urge you to clean your plate because of the "starving kids in China"? As much as we think that pushing kids to eat is a bad idea, her notion to consider those less fortunate has value. Take time to ponder the positive events and people in your life.

- ✔ **Kindnesses:** Think about those who've extended kindness to you.

- ✔ **Education:** Obviously, you can read — a blessing compared to the millions in the world with no chance for an education.

- ✔ **Nourishment:** You probably aren't starving to death, while, as your mother may have noted, millions are.

- ✔ **Home:** Do you live in a cardboard box, or do you have a roof over your head?

- ✔ **Pleasure:** Can you smell flowers, hear birds sing, or touch the soft fur of a pet?

Sources of possible gratitude abound — freedom, health, companionship, and so on. Everyone has a different list. You can find yours by following Corrine's example.

Corrine, a single mother, worries about money, keeping up her house, and especially her children, Trenton, age 15, and Julia, 12. She obsesses about the effect that her divorce has had on her kids and tries to be mother and father as well as teacher and police officer to them. Sometimes she just feels like crying.

When the principal called to tell her that a teacher had caught her son smoking pot in the parking lot, she fell apart. The court ordered counseling for the entire family. The therapist suggested keeping a journal of hassles and blessings for both mother and son Trenton. Look at Corrine's first entries in Table 4-2.

Table 4-2	Corrine's Daily Hassles and Gratitude Journal	
Time of Day	**Hassles**	**Blessings**
Morning	As usual, I had to wake Trenton three or four times, even though his alarm went off earlier. He barely talked to me at breakfast and was almost late for school. I worry so much that he'll fail everything. What would I do then? I want so much for him to be happy in life.	I can at least appreciate the fact that my kids are healthy. We have a nice home, and although I feel strapped sometimes, no one is starving here.
Afternoon	At work, I got put in charge of the new Dudley account. I don't know if I can handle this much responsibility. It makes me nervous just thinking about organizing all the people involved.	Hey, I have a great job and a new promotion. The boss must think I do good work even if I worry about it.

Time of Day	Hassles	Blessings
Evening	Dinner was the usual frozen stir-fry. Trenton didn't come home from practice until everything was cold. Julia watched TV and said little.	I'm grateful for the fact that Trenton is interested in soccer. It will help keep him away from the wrong crowd. Julia is the sweetest kid there ever was, even though she watches too much TV.

Certainly, Corrine needs to work with her son on the incident at school and a few other issues. But when her anxiety rises to extremes, she can't be the parent she wants to be.

Writing in a journal helps Corrine put a different perspective on her problems. She realizes that she's been so uptight about her kids that she hasn't taken the time to notice the good things about them and her own life. Like most people, Corrine has her share of hassles and blessings. Writing about her hassles discharges a little of the emotion she's bottled up about her concerns. Writing about what she feels grateful for helps to counteract some of her negative obsessions.

 Consider keeping a journal as Corrine did. You can use Table 4-2 as a format for your own daily notes. Even if you don't think it could help you, try it for a few days. You might be surprised.

Sizing Up Success

You may feel some benefit from simply rating your anxiety on a daily basis and from journaling, but don't expect large improvements overnight. Change takes time. Sometimes, it takes a number of weeks before a positive direction emerges. After all, you spent much of your life feeling anxious; give change time as well.

You should also know that improvement doesn't happen in a constant, smooth fashion. Rather, it takes a jagged, mountainous course with many ups and downs. You'll have peaks — times when you feel that you're on top of the world and on the verge of conquering your anxiety. But you'll also slip into valleys, and you may feel as though you're on the edge of failure and despair.

Realize that if you're standing in the middle of one of the valleys, it looks like a long climb. You could feel like you're making no progress at all because all you see are peaks. These are not the times for evaluating your progress. But the advantage of a valley is that it can tell you much about what trips you up. If you're in a valley, rather than catastrophize, take the opportunity to reflect and know that things will get better.

If you don't start feeling better after a number of weeks, or if you start feeling utterly hopeless, you should consider seeking professional advice.

Chapter 5

Detecting the Symptoms of Depression

. . . .

In This Chapter

▶ Looking at the symptoms of depression

▶ Discovering depression's many forms

▶ Linking health issues and grief to depression

. . . .

Depression appears in diverse demeanors and guises. Sometimes depression slowly and silently possesses the mind and soul. Other times depression explodes, bursting through the door and robbing its victims of joy and pleasure. Some people are unaware that they have depression, although other people fully recognize depression's presence in their lives. Sometimes depression has no obvious cause, often masquerading as a set of physical complaints like fatigue, poor sleep and appetite, and even indigestion.

Depression is a disease of extremes. Its power can destroy the appetite or create insatiable hunger. People with depression may find sleep distressingly evasive, or they may find that fatigue is overwhelming, confining them to bed for days at a time. Depressed people may pace frantically or collapse and hardly move. Depression sometimes takes root and endures for months or years. Other times it blows through like a series of afternoon thunderstorms.

In this chapter, we help you recognize whether you or someone you care about suffers from depression. We do so by categorizing the effects depression has on individuals. We outline the major types of depression and their symptoms. We also explore the connections between disease and depression, and we look at the grief-depression link.

Recognizing the Ravages of Depression

Everyone feels down from time to time. Stock market plunges, health problems, the loss of a friend, divorce, or failure to reach sales quotas — events like these can make anyone feel sad and upset for a while. But depression is more than a normal reaction to unpleasant events and losses. Depression deepens and spreads well beyond sadness, disrupting both the mind and the body in serious, sometimes deadly ways.

Depression impacts every aspect of life. In fact, even though a number of types of depression exist (see "The Six Plagues of Depression," later in this chapter), all types of depression affect people in four areas, although each individual may be affected in different ways. Depression disrupts

- Thoughts
- Behaviors
- Relationships
- The body

In the following sections, we touch on the ways that each form of depression affects individuals.

Dwelling on bleak thoughts

When you get depressed, your view of the world changes. The sun shines less brightly, the sky clouds over, people seem cold and distant, and the future looks dark. Your mind may cloud over with recurrent thoughts of worthlessness, self-loathing, and even death. Typically, depressed people complain of difficulty concentrating, remembering, and making decisions.

For **Ellen,** depression emerges about one year after her divorce. She finds herself thinking that all men are jerks. Ellen is quite attractive, although when she looks in the mirror, she only sees the beginning of wrinkles and an occasional blemish. She concludes that even if any good men are left, her awful looks will repulse them. She feels tense. Her concentration is shot, and she starts to make careless errors at work. Her boss understands, but she sees her mistakes as proof of incompetence. Although she believes she's in a dead-end job, she doesn't see herself as capable of doing anything better. She begins to wonder why she bothers to go to work every day.

Does your mind dwell on negative thoughts? If so, you may be suffering from depression. The following "Depressive Thoughts Quiz" checklist gives you a sample of typical thoughts that go along with depression. Check the box preceding each thought that you often have:

❑ Things are getting worse and worse for me.

❑ I think I'm worthless.

❑ No one would miss me if I was dead.

❑ My memory is shot.

❑ I make too many mistakes.

❑ By and large, I think I'm a failure.

❑ Lately, I find it impossible to make decisions.

❑ I don't look forward to much of anything.

❑ The world would be a better place without me.

❑ Basically, I'm extremely pessimistic about things.

❑ I can't think of anything that sounds interesting or enjoyable.

❑ My life is full of regrets.

❑ Lately, I can't concentrate, and I forget what I read.

❑ I don't see my life getting better in the future.

❑ I'm deeply ashamed of myself.

Unlike many of the self-tests you may have seen in magazines or books, no specific score indicates depression here. All the items are typical of depressed thinking. However, merely checking one or two doesn't necessarily mean you're depressed. But the more items you check, the greater the concern of possible depression. And if you check any of the items related to death or suicide, that's plenty of cause for concern.

If you're having serious suicidal thoughts, you need an immediate evaluation and treatment. If the thoughts include a plan that you believe you may actually carry out now or in the very near future, go to a hospital emergency room, where trained personnel can help you. If you're unable to get yourself to an emergency room, call 911 for more rapid attention.

Depressed behavior

Not everyone who's depressed behaves in the same way. Some people speed up, and others slow down. Some folks sleep more than ever, while others complain of a dreadful lack of sleep.

Darryl drags his body out of bed in the morning. Even after ten hours of sleep, he feels depleted of energy. He starts showing up at work late. He uses up his sick leave. He can't make himself go to the gym, an activity he used to enjoy. He reasons that he'll work out again when he gets the energy. His friends ask him what's going on, because he hasn't been spending much time with them. He says that he doesn't really know; he's just tired.

Cheryl, on the other hand, is averaging about three and a half hours of sleep each night. She awakens at about 3 a.m. with racing thoughts. When she gets up, she feels a frantic pressure and can't seem to sit still. Irritable and cranky, she snaps at her friends and coworkers. Unable to sleep at night, she finds herself drinking too much. Sometimes she cries for no apparent reason.

Although everyone is different, certain behaviors tend to go along with depression. Do your actions and behaviors concern you? Depressed people tend to either feel like they're walking in wet cement or running full speed on a treadmill. The following "Depressed Behavior Quiz" checklist can give you an idea whether your actions indicate a problem. Check each item that applies to you:

❑ I've been having unexplained crying spells.

❑ The few times I force myself to go out, I don't have much fun.

❑ I can't make myself exercise like I used to.

❑ I haven't been going out nearly as much as usual.

❑ I've been missing a lot of work lately.

❑ I can't get myself to do much of anything, even important projects.

❑ Lately I've been fidgety and can't sit still.

❑ I'm moving at a slower pace than I usually do, for no good reason.

❑ I haven't been doing things for fun like I usually do.

All the preceding behaviors are typical of depressed behavior or, in some cases, a health problem. On a bad day, anyone might check off a single item. However, the more items you check, the more likely something's wrong, especially if your problem exists for more than a couple of weeks.

Reflecting on relationships and depression

Depression damages the way you relate to others. Withdrawal and avoidance are the most common responses to depression. Sometimes depressed people get irritable and critical with the very people they care most about.

Trent trips over a toy left on the living room floor and snaps at his wife, Sylvia, "Can't you get the kids to pick up their damn toys for once?" Hurt and surprised by the attack, Sylvia apologizes. Trent fails to acknowledge her apology and turns away. Sylvia quickly picks up the toy and wonders what's been happening to her marriage. Trent hardly talks to her anymore, other than to complain or scold her about something trivial. She can't remember the last time they had sex. She worries that he may be having an affair.

Have you or perhaps someone you care about been responding differently in one or more of your relationships? The following "Depression and Relationships Quiz" checklist describes some of the ways in which depression affects relationships. Check the items that fit your situation:

❑ I've been avoiding people more than usual, including friends and family.

❑ I've been having more difficulty than usual talking about my concerns.

❑ I've been unusually irritable with others.

❑ I don't feel like being with anyone.

❑ I feel isolated and alone.

❑ I'm sure that no one cares about or understands me.

❑ I haven't felt like being physically intimate with anyone lately.

❑ I feel like I've been letting down those who are close to me.

❑ I believe that others don't want to be around me.

❑ Lately, I don't seem to care about anyone like I should.

When you're depressed, you turn away from the very people that may have the most support to offer you. Either you feel that they don't care about you, or perhaps you can't muster up positive feelings for them. You may avoid others or find yourself irritated and crabby.

The more items you checked in the previous list, the more likely depression is affecting your relationships.

The physical signs of depression

Depression typically includes at least a few physical symptoms, which include changes in appetite, sleep, and energy. However, for some people, the experience of depression *primarily* consists of physical symptoms and doesn't consciously include as many other symptoms, such as sadness, withdrawal from people, lack of interests, and missed work.

 Many folks who experience depression primarily in physical terms are very unaware of their emotional life. Sometimes, that's because they were taught that feelings are unimportant. In other cases, their parents scolded them for crying or showing other appropriate feelings, such as excitement or sadness.

When **Carl** was growing up, his father scolded him for crying. He said that big boys tough things out and that Carl should never show weakness. His father also jumped on him for showing too much excitement in anticipation of Christmas. He said that men don't get emotional. Over time, Carl learned to keep his feelings to himself.

After five years of marriage, Carl's wife leaves him; she says that he's an unfeeling and uncaring man. In the ensuing six months, Carl finds his appetite diminished, and food no longer tastes good to him. His energy drains away like oil from an engine when the oil pan plug is removed. He starts to have headaches and frequent bouts of constipation. His blood pressure even rises.

When he goes to the clinic, his doctor asks, "Look Carl, your wife left you just six months ago. Are you sure you aren't depressed?" Carl answers, "Are you kidding? Depression is something women get. I couldn't possibly be depressed." Nonetheless, after an exhaustive work-up, his doctor concludes that depression is causing Carl's physical problems. Nothing else adds up.

 Are you experiencing odd changes in your body that you have no explanation for? The following "Depression in the Body Quiz" checklist shows you some of the various ways that depression can show up in your body:

❑ My blood pressure has risen lately for no discernable reason.

❑ I have no appetite lately.

❑ I haven't been sleeping nearly as well as usual.

❑ My diet is the same, but I'm having frequent constipation for no reason.

❑ I often feel sick to my stomach.

❑ I feel lots of aches and pains.

❑ I'm sleeping much more than usual.

❑ I've been ravenous lately for no reason.

❑ My energy has been very low lately.

❑ I've gained (or lost) more than 5 pounds, and I can't figure out why.

Like the other three checklists in this chapter, it really doesn't matter exactly how many of the preceding physical symptoms apply to you. The more items you checked, the greater the possibility of depression.

If your depression shows up primarily in physical terms, medications or some other physical remedy may seem like the best choice of treatment for you.

The items in this checklist may be caused by other health-related problems, not just depression. Therefore, if you're experiencing any disturbing physical problems, you need to see your doctor, especially if they last more than a week or two.

The Six Plagues of Depression

In the "Recognizing the Ravages of Depression" section, earlier in this chapter, we outline the four broad ways all types of depression can affect an individual. In this section, we turn our attention to the six major types of depression to look out for:

- ✔ Major depressive disorder
- ✔ Dysthymic disorder
- ✔ Adjustment disorder with depressed mood
- ✔ Bipolar disorder
- ✔ Seasonal affective disorder
- ✔ Depression related to hormones

The American Psychiatric Association publishes a book called the *Diagnostic and Statistical Manual of Mental Disorders* (DSM-IV). The DSM-IV describes and categorizes mental disorders. In the following sections, we describe six major types of depression and their symptoms, largely based on information contained in the DSM-IV. However, we present this information in a condensed format without technical jargon.

Understanding what the forms of depression look like can help you figure out whether you're likely suffering from some type of depression. But don't go so far as to give yourself a formal diagnosis; that's a job for professionals.

If you feel that you have significant signs of any of these types of depression, get help. You can start with the advice in this book, but if you don't feel much better within a couple of months, see your doctor or a mental health professional. Seek help even sooner if your depression includes serious thoughts of suicide or hopelessness.

Major depressive disorder

As with all types of depression, the symptoms of a major depressive disorder fall into the four areas we cover in the "Recognizing the Ravages of Depression" section earlier in this chapter — thoughts, behaviors, relationships, and the body. So what's unique about a major depressive disorder?

Major depressive disorders involve either a seriously low mood or a notable drop in pleasures and interests that unrelentingly continues for two weeks or more. Sometimes depressed people, either consciously or unconsciously, deny their down feelings and declines in interests. In cases of denial, careful observation by people who know them well usually detects the impairment.

In addition to the low mood and lack of pleasure, in order to qualify as experiencing a major depressive disorder, you generally have to have a wide variety of other symptoms, such as

- ✔ Inability to concentrate or make decisions
- ✔ Repetitive thoughts of suicide
- ✔ Major changes in sleep patterns
- ✔ Extreme fatigue
- ✔ Clear signs of either revved-up agitation or slowed functioning
- ✔ Very low sense of personal worth

✔ Striking changes in appetite or weight (either increased or decreased)

✔ Intense feelings of guilt and self-condemnation

With major depressive disorders, the preceding symptoms occur almost every day over a period of at least two weeks. Major depressive disorders vary greatly in terms of severity. However, even mild cases need treatment.

 The degree of despondency people with severe cases of major depressive disorder experience is difficult to imagine for someone who has never experienced it. A severe, major episode of depression grabs hold of a person's life and insidiously squeezes out all pleasure. But it does far more than obliterate joy; severe depression shoves its victims into a dark hole of utter, unrelenting despair that obscures the capacity to love. People caught in such a web of depression lose the ability to care for life, others, and themselves.

 If you suffer from such a severe case of depression, you have reason to hope. Many effective treatments work even with severe depression.

The daily pain of living begins the moment the alarm wakes **Edwin** up. He spends most of the night tossing and turning. He only falls asleep for a few moments before waking up to another day of despair. He forces himself to get ready for work, but the thought of speaking to others feels overwhelming. He can't face the prospect. He knows that he should at least call in sick but can't lift his hand to pick up the phone. He realizes that he could lose his job, but it doesn't seem to matter. He thinks he's likely to be dead soon.

He changes out of his work clothes and into sweats; then he goes back to bed. But he doesn't sleep. His

mind fills with thoughts of self-loathing — "I'm a failure. I'm no good. There's nothing to live for." He ponders whether he should just end it now. Edwin suffers
from a major depressive disorder.

Major depressive disorders generally cause a
sharply reduced ability to function at work or
deal with other people. In other words, such disorders deplete you of the resources you need for
recovery, which is why getting help is so important. If you allow the major depressive disorder
to continue, it may result in death from suicide. If
you or someone you know *even suspects* the presence of a major depressive disorder, you need to
seek help promptly. See Chapter 7 for ideas on
how to find professional help for depression.

Major, major depression

Psychosis is a serious symptom of a major depressive disorder in which a person is out of touch with reality. People
with depression sometimes become so ill that they become
psychotic. They may hear voices or see things that aren't
really there. In most instances, depression with psychosis
requires hospitalization.

People with severe depression also may exhibit paranoid or
delusional thinking. *Paranoid thinking* involves feeling
extremely suspicious and distrustful — such as believing
that other people are out to get you or that someone is trying
to poison you. *Delusions* range from the slightly odd to the
bizarre, but they involve obviously false beliefs, such as
thinking the television is transmitting signals to your brain.
The problems of psychosis, paranoia, and delusional thinking require professional attention and lie outside of the
scope of this book.

Dysthymic disorder

Dysthymic disorder, or *dysthymia,* looks rather similar to major depressive disorder. However, it's generally considered somewhat less severe and tends to be more chronic. With dysthymic disorder, the symptoms occur for at least two years (oftentimes far longer), with the depressed mood appearing on most days for the majority of each day. However, you only need to display two of the following chronic symptoms, in addition to a depressed mood, in order for your condition to qualify as a dysthymic disorder:

- ✔ Poor concentration
- ✔ Low sense of personal worth
- ✔ Guilty feelings
- ✔ Thoughts of death or suicide
- ✔ Problems making decisions

Compared to major depressive disorder, dysthymic disorder less frequently involves prominent physical symptoms, such as difficulties with appetite, weight, sleep, and agitation.

Dysthymic disorder frequently begins in childhood, adolescence, or young adulthood and can easily continue for many years if left untreated. Furthermore, individuals with dysthymic disorder carry an increased risk of developing a major depressive disorder at some point in their lives.

Although individuals with dysthymic disorder don't appear as devastatingly despondent as those with a major depressive disorder, they nonetheless languish, lacking in vigor and joie de vivre. You may not identify people with dysthymic disorder as depressed, but they sure seem pessimistic and perhaps cynical and grouchy a good deal of the time.

Charlene doesn't remember ever feeling joy. She's not even sure what the word means. Her parents worked long hours and seemed cold and distant. Charlene studied hard in school. She hoped to gain approval and attention for her academic accomplishments, but her parents didn't seem to notice.

Today, Charlene leads a life her colleagues envy. She earns a great salary and toils tirelessly in her profession as a mechanical engineer. Yet she senses that she's missing something, feels unsuccessful, and suffers a chronic, uneasy discontent. Charlene has a ysthymic disorder, although she won't say she's depressed. She fails to seek help for her problem because she actually has no idea that life can be different.

People with dysthymic disorder often see their problems as merely "just the way they are" and fail to seek treatment. If you suspect that you or someone you care about has dysthymic disorder, get help. You have the right to feel better than you do, and the long-lasting nature of the problem means it isn't likely to go away on its own. Besides, you certainly don't want to risk developing a major depressive disorder, which is even more debilitating.

Adjustment disorder with depressed mood

Life isn't a bowl of cherries. Bad things do happen to everyone from time to time. Sometimes people handle their problems without excess emotional upset. Sometimes they don't.

Adjustment disorders are reactions to one or more difficult issues, such as marital problems, financial setbacks, conflicts with coworkers, or natural disasters. When a stressful event occurs and your reaction includes a decreased ability to work or participate effectively with others, in combination with symptoms such as a low mood, crying spells, and feelings of worthlessness or hopelessness, you may be experiencing an adjustment disorder with a depressed mood. Adjustment disorder is a much milder problem than a major depressive disorder, but it can still disrupt your life.

James is shocked when his boss tells him that due to downsizing, he's losing his job. He begins a job search, but openings in his field are scarce. For the first couple of weeks, he enjoys catching up on sleep, but soon he starts feeling unusually down. He struggles to open up the newspaper to look for work. He begins to feel worthless and loses hope of finding a job. His appetite and sleep are still okay, but his confidence plummets. He's surprised when tears stream down his face after receiving another rejection letter.

James isn't suffering from a major depressive disorder. James is struggling with an adjustment disorder with depressed mood.

Bipolar disorder: Ups and downs

Bipolar disorder is considered a mood disorder, just like other forms of depression. However, bipolar disorder is quite different from other depressions because people with bipolar disorder always experience one or more episodes of unusually euphoric feelings, referred to as *mania*.

In bipolar disorder, moods tend to fluctuate between extreme highs and lows, making the treatment of bipolar disorder different from most depressions. We want you to be familiar with the symptoms so that you can seek professional help if you experience manic episodes with your depression. Self-help isn't sufficient for the treatment of bipolar disorder.

Although individuals with mania may seem quite cheerful and happy, the people who know them can tell that their good mood is a little too good to be true. During manic episodes, people need less sleep, may show signs of unusual creativity, and have more energy and enthusiasm. Sounds like a pretty nice mood to have, doesn't it? Who wouldn't want to feel wonderful and totally on top of the world? Well, hold the phone.

The problem with manic episodes related to bipolar disorder is that the high feelings spin out of control. During these episodes, good judgment goes out the window. People who have this disorder often

✔ Spend too much money

✔ Gamble excessively

✔ Make foolish business decisions

✔ Engage in risky sexual escapades

✔ Talk fast and furiously

✔ Think that they have super-special talents or abilities

Manic episodes can involve mildly foolish decisions and excesses, or they can reach extreme levels. People in manic states can cause ruin for themselves or their families. Their behavior can get so out of control that they end up in the hospital for a period of time.

Most people with bipolar disorder also cycle into episodes of mild to severe depression. They go from feeling great to gruesome, occasionally within the same day. The depressions that follow a manic episode feel especially unexpected and devastating. The contrast from the high to the low is particularly painful. People with untreated bipolar disorder typically feel out of control, hopeless, and helpless. Not surprisingly, the risk of suicide is higher for bipolar disorder than for any of the other types of depression.

Although it's generally chronic, bipolar disorder can be successfully managed. Both medications and psychotherapy, usually in combination, can alleviate many of the most debilitating symptoms. Scientists are continually developing new treatments and medications.

Emily finishes dressing, grabs her keys, and dashes out the door. She feels so excited that she can hardly wait to share her good fortune with her girlfriend Samantha. "Sam, guess what," she gushes, "I've finally decided to move to L.A. I know that I can make it in the movies. I just have to go. I've quit my job and I'm going. As a matter of fact, I'm leaving today."

Emily's fast talking frightens Samantha. She asks Emily when she decided to move and what she's going to do about the lease on her apartment; does she have a job offer in L.A. — what is she thinking? This is so sudden.

Emily replies that she hasn't been able to sleep for the past three days. Her thoughts have been racing with ideas. She decided that her life is too boring and she needs a change. She says that her boss can go to hell and so can the apartment manager. She charged the plane ticket and took her last $200 from her bank account. She's going to figure out what to do when she gets to L.A. Emily suffers from bipolar disorder.

Bipolar disorder is a complicated, serious syndrome. The condition has many subtle variations. If you suspect that you or someone you know has any signs of bipolar disorder, seek professional assistance immediately.

Seasonal affective disorder

Some depressions come and go with the seasons, just like clockwork. People who regularly experience depression during the fall or winter may have *seasonal affective disorder* (SAD). People who have SAD may also experience a few unusual symptoms, such as

- ✔ Increased appetite
- ✔ Carbohydrate cravings
- ✔ Increased sleep
- ✔ Irritability
- ✔ A sense of heaviness in the arms and legs

Many mental health professionals believe that the reduced amount of sunlight in the winter triggers SAD in vulnerable individuals. Support for this hypothesis comes from the fact that this pattern of depression occurs more frequently among people who live in higher latitudes, where light fluctuations from winter to summer are most extreme and darkness prevails for a greater portion of the day during the winter.

What does a bear do to get ready for winter? Bears frantically forage for food, get as fat as they can, and hibernate in a cozy cave. Perhaps it's not a coincidence that people with SAD typically gain weight, crave carbohydrates, have reduced energy, and feel like staying swaddled in bed for the winter.

Premenstrual dysphoric disorder and postpartum depression

Occasional, minor premenstrual changes in mood occur in a majority of women. A smaller percentage of women experience significant and disturbing symptoms known as *premenstrual dysphoric disorder* (PDD). PDD is a more extreme form of the more widely known premenstrual syndrome (PMS).

Although hormones likely play a significant role in PDD, research hasn't yet clarified the causes. Typically, women who suffer from full-blown PDD encounter some of the following symptoms almost every month during the week prior to menstruation. (These same symptoms can occur — most likely from hormonal fluctuations — over the years leading up to, during, and following menopause.)

- Anger
- Anxiety
- Bloating
- Fatigue
- Food cravings
- Guilt and self-blame
- Irritability
- Sadness
- Tearfulness
- Withdrawal

Denise drives to the grocery store after work. Impatiently, she pushes her cart through the aisle, only to find another patron blocking her way. She feels a rush of annoyance and clears her throat loudly. The other woman looks up and apologizes. Denise hurriedly works her way around the offending cart, giving it a quick shove as she passes.

Waiting in line, her irascible mood worsens. The man in front of her fumbles around for his checkbook and discovers he has no checks. Then he pulls out a handful of cash and realizes he's a bit short. Next, he starts to search his overstuffed wallet for a credit card.

Denise finds herself unable to suppress her raging emotions and snaps, "People don't have all day to stand in line waiting for clods like you! What's wrong with you, anyway?"

The man's face turns bright red, and he mutters, "Gosh, I'm sorry lady." The clerk intervenes and says, "Wow ma'am. You don't have to be so mean. It can happen to anybody." Suddenly ashamed, Denise breaks into tears and sobs. She feels like she's going crazy. And this isn't the first time Denise has felt this way. In fact, it happens to her almost on a monthly basis.

Postpartum depression is another type of serious mood disorder that's widely thought to be related to hormonal fluctuations, although no one knows for sure how and why the hormones profoundly affect the moods of some women and not others. This depression occurs within days or weeks after giving birth. The symptoms appear quite similar to those of major depressive disorder. (For a complete discussion of these symptoms, see the "Major depressive disorder" section, earlier in this chapter.)

Carmen had tried unsuccessfully to conceive for the past eight years. She and her husband Shawn feel overwhelmed with joy when at last the home pregnancy test registers positive. Their cheerful, cozy nursery looks like a picture in a baby magazine.

Carmen and Shawn weep with happiness at the sight of their newborn. Carmen feels exhausted, but Shawn assumes that's normal. He takes charge the first day home so that Carmen can rest. Carmen feels the same way the next day, so Shawn continues to take over the responsibilities of caring for the baby. Shawn becomes alarmed when Carmen shows no interest in holding the baby. In fact, she seems irritated by the baby's crying and mentions that maybe she shouldn't have become a mother. At the end of the second week, she tells him that he can't go back to work because she doesn't think she can take care of the baby. Carmen is suffering from postpartum depression.

 Most women feel a little bit of postpartum depression, or the "baby blues," shortly after delivery. It's not severe and usually dissipates in a couple of weeks. However, if you begin to feel like Carmen in the previous story, you need to get professional help immediately.

Connecting Drugs, Diseases, and Depression

The interaction of depression with illness and disease can be a vicious cycle. Illness and disease (and related medications) can hasten the onset or intensify the effects of depression. And depression can further complicate various diseases. Depression can suppress the immune system, release stress hormones, and impact your body and mind's capacity to cope. Depression may increase whatever pain you have and further rob you of crucial resources. In this section, we focus on the role of medications and illness in the development and worsening of depression.

Depressing drugs

Dealing with an illness is hard enough without having medications make you feel even worse, but some medications actually appear to cause depression. Of course, sometimes distinguishing whether it's merely being sick or the drug that's causing the depression is difficult. However, in a number of cases, medications do appear to contribute directly to depression.

If you notice inexplicable feelings of sadness shortly after starting a new medication, tell your doctor. The medication could be causing your feelings, and an alternative treatment that won't make you depressed may be available. Table 5-1 lists the most common offending medications.

Table 5-1	Potentially Depressing Drugs
Medication	*Condition Typically Prescribed For*
Antabuse	Alcohol addiction
Anticonvulsants	Seizures
Barbiturates	Seizures and (rarely) anxiety
Benzodiazepines	Anxiety and insomnia
Beta blockers	High blood pressure and heart problems
Calcium channel blockers	High blood pressure and heart problems
Corticosteroids	Inflammation and chronic lung diseases
Hormones	Birth control and menopausal symptoms
Interferon	Hepatitis and certain cancers
Levodopa, amantadine	Parkinson's disease
Statins	High cholesterol
Zovirax	Herpes or shingles

Depressing diseases

Chronic illnesses interfere with life. Some chronic illnesses require lifestyle adjustments, extensive time at the doctor's office, missed work, disrupted relationships, and pain. Feeling upset by such disturbances is normal. But these problems may trigger depression, especially in vulnerable people.

In addition, certain specific diseases seem to disrupt the nervous system in ways that create depression. If you suffer from one of these diseases, talk to your doctor if your mood begins to deteriorate. Diseases that are thought to directly influence depression include

- AIDS
- Asthma
- Cancer
- Chronic fatigue syndrome
- Coronary artery disease and heart attacks
- Diabetes
- Hepatitis
- Lupus
- Multiple sclerosis
- Parkinson's disease
- Stroke
- Ulcerative colitis

Good Grief! Is Depression Ever Normal?

When you lose someone you love, you likely feel pain and sadness. You may lose sleep and withdraw from people. The idea of going out and having a good time probably sounds repugnant. Feelings like these can go on for weeks or a few months, but are they signs of depression? Yes and no.

 Although grieving involves many of the same reactions associated with depression, the two aren't the same. Depression almost always includes a diminished sense of personal worth or feelings of excessive guilt. Grief, when not accompanied by depression, doesn't typically involve lowered self-esteem and unreasonable self-blame. Furthermore, the intensity of grief usually diminishes slowly (sometimes excruciatingly slowly) but surely over time. Depression, on the other hand, sometimes holds on unrelentingly.

A controversy exists among some mental health professionals concerning how to best deal with grief. Some professionals advocate immediate treatment of any disturbing reactions involving grief; these professionals often advise taking antidepressant medications. Others contend that grief involves a natural healing process best dealt with by allowing its natural course to unfold.

We tend to agree with the latter group, but if and only if the grief isn't complicated by an accompanying depression. Still, the decision is an individual choice. In either case, a grieving person needs to be aware that depression can superimpose itself on top of grief. If you're dealing with grief, seek treatment if it goes on too long or includes other serious symptoms of depression.

Chapter 6

Tracking the Causes of Your Depression

● ●

In This Chapter

▶ Understanding the causes of depression

▶ Keeping track of your moods

● ●

*I*n this chapter, we delve into the causes of depression and tell you how you or a loved one can monitor and track your moods if you suspect you may be battling depression. For details on detecting the symptoms of depression, see Chapter 5.

Digging Out the Causes of Depression

Lots of theories on the cause of depression exist. Some experts purport that imbalances in brain chemistry cause depression. Advocates of this position sometimes believe that those imbalances in chemistry are due to genetics. Other experts emphatically declare that the cause of depression lies in one's childhood. Still other investigators make the claim that depression comes from negative thinking. You can also find professionals who suggest that depression is caused by impoverished environments and/or cultural experiences. Other researchers have implicated learned patterns of behavior as a cause of depression. Finally, some experts have identified problems with relationships as the major culprit.

In one sense, you can probably come to the same conclusion as the dodo bird in *Alice in Wonderland* and declare that "All have won and all must have prizes." In another sense, nobody deserves a prize. Even though you can find evidence to support each of these positions, nobody truly knows how these factors work, which is the most important, and which ones influence other factors in what ways.

In spite of the indisputable fact that scientists don't yet know exactly how the multitude of depression-related factors function and interact, you may run into doctors, psychologists, and psychiatrists who have strong opinions about what they believe is "the" definitive cause of depression. If you encounter a professional who claims to know the single, definitive cause of depression, question that professional's credibility. Most sophisticated experts in the field of depression research know that a single, definitive cause of depression remains elusive and likely will never be discovered.

Yet the field of mental health isn't clueless when it comes to understanding how depression develops. Strong suggestive evidence supports the fact that learning, thinking, biology, genetics, childhood, and the environment play important roles in the development, maintenance, and potential treatment of depression. All these factors interact in amazing ways.

The brain's brew

About 100 billion *neurons* (nerve cells) reside in your brain, give or take a few. Busy neurons take in information about the state of the world outside and inside the body. These 100 billion nerve cells don't touch each other. They send information back and forth by spitting out tiny molecules. This communication process involves chemical messengers called *neurotransmitters* that move through and between the neurons.

Evidence shows that chemical imbalances in the brain either accompany or cause depression. Several theories have been offered to explain the relationship between depression and the chemical messengers. Many researchers believe that neurotransmitters such as norepinephrine, serotonin, and dopamine play important, interactive roles in mood regulation. Furthermore, these neurotransmitters may interact with other brain chemicals in as yet unknown ways.

What researchers do know is that for some people with depression, the chemical soup may need a dash of salt (one medication), and for others, pepper (a different medication) may be necessary to alleviate the depression. But that doesn't necessarily mean a lack of pepper or salt caused the depression! Experts simply don't know how all this works.

For example, a growing body of studies has shown that medication alters the physical symptoms of depression, such as loss of appetite and energy. Antidepressant medication also improves the negative, pessimistic thinking that accompanies most forms of depression. Perhaps that's not too surprising.

Similarly, studies have demonstrated that psychotherapy alone decreases negative, pessimistic thinking much like medications do. Some scientists are shocked by the fact that other studies now demonstrate that certain psychotherapies, even if delivered without antidepressant medication, also alter brain chemistry.

Taken as a whole, recent studies on the roots of depression fail to support a theory that assigns one specific cause of depression. Rather, they support the idea that physical and psychological factors interact with each other.

Monitoring Mood

You may be pretty sure that you or someone you care about has depression. Now what? Keeping track of how your mood changes from day to day is one important step in recovery. Why?

- ✔ You may discover patterns (perhaps you get very depressed every Monday).

- ✔ You may discover specific triggers for your depressed moods.

- ✔ You can see how your efforts progress over time.

- ✔ You can quickly determine if you're not progressing, which may indicate that you need to seek help.

We suggest that you keep a "Mood Diary" (see Table 6-1). You can profit from tracking your moods and taking notes on relevant incidents, happenings, and thoughts. Try it for a few weeks.

Use a rating scale from 1 to 100 to rate your mood each day (or at multiple times throughout the day). A rating of 100 means that you feel ecstatic. You feel on top of the world, maybe like you just won $80 million or received the Nobel Peace Prize — whatever turns you on. A rating of 50 means just a regular day. Your mood is acceptable — nothing special, nothing bad. A rating of 1 is just about the worst day imaginable. Interestingly, we find that most people without depression rate their average mood at around 70, even though we define 50 as middle range.

In addition to your mood rating, jot down a few notes about your day. Include anything that may relate to your mood, such as

- ✔ Clashes with friends, coworkers, or lovers
- ✔ Difficult times of the day
- ✔ Falling in love
- ✔ Financial difficulties
- ✔ Loneliness
- ✔ Negative thoughts or daydreams floating through your mind
- ✔ An unexpected promotion
- ✔ Wonderful weather
- ✔ Work hassles

John suspects that he may have a problem, so he tracks his mood and finds a few interesting patterns. For an example of one week in John's mood diary, check out Table 6-1.

Table 6-1		Weekly Mood Diary
Day	*Mood Rating*	*Notes (Events or Thoughts, for Example)*
Sunday	20	Not a good day. I hung out and worried about getting my quarterly tax payment together by Thursday. And I felt horribly guilty about letting the lawn go without mowing it.
Monday	30 (a.m.) 45 (p.m.)	The day started miserably. I got stuck in traffic and was late for work. In the afternoon, things seemed to go more smoothly, although I can't say I felt on top of the world.
Tuesday	40	Nothing good, nothing bad today. Just the blahs.
Wednesday	30 (a.m.) 40 (p.m.)	I woke up feeling panicked about the new project deadline. I don't know how I'll ever get it done. By the afternoon I'd made a little progress, but I still worried about it.
Thursday	35 (a.m.) 45 (p.m.)	I was thinking about the fact that the days just seem to drag on. I don't look forward to much. In the evening, I enjoyed a phone conversation with a friend.

Day	Mood Rating	Notes (Events or Thoughts, for Example)
Friday	50	Miraculously, I got the project done four hours early. My boss said it was the greatest thing he'd ever seen me do. Of course, he probably doesn't think much about my other work.
Saturday	40	I finally got the grass cut. That felt good, but then I had too much time on my hands and started to worry again.

John studies several weeks of his mood diaries. He notices that he usually feels morose on Sunday afternoons. He realizes that, on Sunday, he typically spends time alone and mulls over imagined difficulties of the upcoming week. He also discovers that mornings aren't exactly the best time of the day because he worries about the rest of the day. Interestingly, he also discovers that his worries often involve catastrophic predictions (like not meeting deadlines) that rarely come true. Finally, his mood improves when he tackles projects he's been putting off, like mowing the lawn.

 You can track your progress whether you're working on your own or with a professional. If your progress bogs down, please seek help or discuss the problem with your therapist.

Chapter 7

Finding Help for Depression

*A*re you feeling blue? Okay, we're going to guess that because you're reading this book, you or someone you love feels depressed to some degree. Perhaps you merely feel a little down in the dumps, or maybe you're desperately despondent. The good news is that you can find help in a number of places, from the bookstore to the therapist's office. The bad news is that the shear number of choices can confuse the issue. In this chapter, we clear up the confusion by laying out your options for obtaining help and giving you the tools you need to make an informed decision.

We provide you with background information on three primary options for dealing with depression — self-help, psychotherapy, and medication — so you

can figure out what's right for you. We help you deci-
pher the differences among various mental health
professionals and determine whether you have a
good match with the professional you choose.

Stumbling onto a Solution

People often neglect to think through their decision
to seek help or investigate their options carefully.
Sometimes this approach works out just fine — even
though the options for dealing with depression are
numerous and strikingly different.

Consider **Betty,** for example. She takes a job as a head
librarian in a new city. She feels excited about her
new position. Nevertheless, she misses her friends
and family far more than she expected. At the age of
52, she's considerably older than her coworkers, and
she finds it difficult to relate to them. After talking to
her adult daughter on the phone one evening, she's
surprised to find tears welling up in her eyes. Over
the next few weeks, her mood deteriorates, and she
begins to cry frequently. She feels rising guilt and
remorse for having moved away from the ones she
loves.

Betty receives a new shipment of books and notices
one about fighting depression. She begins to leaf
through it. The book's message resonates with her.
After reading a few chapters, she concludes that her
mood reflects an adjustment disorder with depressed
mood. Over the next six weeks, she picks the book up
many times and tries out its many suggestions. Her
mood gradually brightens, and she starts to enjoy her
new job and new city.

Betty stumbled upon the self-help option, and it
worked for her. Other folks find their way into therapy
or medication, and they meet with great success.

(Believe it or not, people with depression usually deal with it successfully when they seek reasonable help.)

Many people don't just luck out and find the best option to deal with their depression. A more surefire approach is to really consider all your options for help and weigh the information carefully to make the best choice for you.

Exploring the Self-Help Option

Everyone who's dealing with depression can benefit from self-help. *Self-help* refers to efforts you make on your own, without professional assistance, to deal with your depression. Scores of studies have demonstrated the value of self-help for a variety of emotional, behavioral, and medical difficulties. For some individuals, self-help appears to be all they need. However, self-help may not be enough. Even if your own efforts fall short, self-help can provide a potent addition to therapy, medication, or a combination of both.

Deciding whether self-help is a singular solution

Should you consider self-help as an exclusive means of overcoming your depression? Before making the decision to try self-help alone as your strategy, ask yourself the following questions:

✔ **Am I having any suicidal thoughts?** If the answer is "yes," you need to obtain an evaluation from a mental health professional. That person will likely recommend psychotherapy, medication, or a combination of the two in addition to self-help.

✔ **Is my depression seriously interfering with my life in areas such as work, relationships, sleep, appetite, or recreation?** Once again, if the answer is "yes," you may be suffering from a major depressive disorder (see Chapter 5 for more information), which means that you probably need more than just self-help.

If you answer "no" to both of the preceding questions, self-help may be the right place to start. However, you need to consider another question before you begin: "Do I have the desire and motivation to work on the advice I receive from self-help sources?" We're not talking about hours of study every day. But self-help does require more than a quick read of an article or book. And you, like plenty of folks, may do better when you have a coach or leader inspiring you. Only you can answer this question. If you can't confidently answer "yes," talk to a mental health professional about your options.

If you make the decision to stick with self-help — great. This book is a terrific place to start. Then, if you want to obtain extra self-help resources, you can choose additional books, videos, self-help groups, or whatever combination of resources you think will help. Work for a while at applying what you learn and monitor your progress carefully. You can use the mood-monitoring form (the "Mood Diary") that we outline in Chapter 6 to help keep track of your improvement.

If you don't see progress through self-help after a couple of months of effort, look into additional assistance. If at any point you feel discouraged, start having suicidal thoughts, or your depression worsens, get additional help. See the "Discovering who's who in psychotherapy" section, later in this chapter, for more information on mental health professionals.

Reviewing the resources

Choosing the right self-help approach depends in part on your personal preferences and style. The fact that you're already reading this book suggests that the written word may appeal to you. The following list covers the most common self-help options:

✔ **Books:** This is the only book in the entire literary world that has value in helping people with depression. Just kidding, folks! Reading several different self-help books is a pretty good idea. Even though you may hear some suggestions more than once, repetition helps you remember, and all authors have slightly different ways of explaining concepts. The best books for dealing with depression give you information about treatments known to work (such as cognitive therapy, behavior therapy, interpersonal therapy, and medication).

Books are an inexpensive way of getting help, which is an obvious advantage. But more importantly, books can also provide you with a whole lot of information that would take a therapist many sessions to cover. And you can refer to the information as often as you need. Finally, if you combine reading with therapy, it may just take you less time to get better.

Make sure that the authors of any self-help book you purchase have credentials and experience helping others deal with depression. (We cover the credentials issue in the "Discovering who's who in psychotherapy" section, later in this chapter.)

✔ **Tapes and videos:** For folks who learn best by hearing or seeing, tapes and videos have merit. Look for the same author credentials and information on effective approaches that we note for books.

✓ **Self-help groups:** Self-help groups offer support and understanding. People with common problems gather in these groups to share information and experiences. Members help themselves and each other by expressing feelings and solving problems together. Unfortunately, we don't know of any major, organized groups like Alcoholics Anonymous or Take Off Pounds Sensibly with a nationwide network of self-help groups for people with depression. However, the National Alliance for the Mentally Ill (Internet: www.nami.org) is a self-help support and advocacy group for people with emotional problems and their families. The group offers information concerning the availability of local support groups. In addition, your local chapter of the United Way likely has a directory of community resources.

✓ **Web sites:** You can find a wide range of resources related to depression on the Internet. You can join a chat room or download articles. However, the Internet has more than its share of unqualified, though well-meaning individuals serving up advice. Outright frauds also market their products and ideas on the Internet.

Numerous unscrupulous entrepreneurs hawk various types of books, tapes, herbs, videos, and other types of merchandise that promise prompt relief from depression with little or no effort. Buyers beware! No miracle cures exist for overcoming depression.

Pursuing the Psychotherapy Option

Psychotherapy involves working with a therapist using psychological techniques to alleviate emotional problems. Psychotherapy works well for treating depression. Incredibly, psychotherapy comes in literally hundreds of different forms and types; a wide array of professionals also practice it. Yikes! How are you ever going to figure out how to get the help you need in this maze of options?

Never fear. In this section, we give you the information you need to find your way through the maze. First, we discuss the types of psychotherapy that are known to work for treating depression, and then we tell you how to sort out who's who among mental health professionals.

Uncovering the effective therapies

Feel free to read the vast literature that encompasses hundreds and hundreds of articles on the effectiveness of psychotherapy for treating depression. We're guessing that you probably don't want to read all that info, so we did the research for you. (Don't feel too bad for us; it's our job.)

The following therapies have been proven to be effective and produce excellent results within a reasonable time frame:

✓ **Cognitive therapy:** In brief, cognitive therapy operates on the assumption that the ways in which people think about, perceive, and interpret events plays a pivotal role in how they feel. For the treatment of depression, no psychotherapy has received as much support as cognitive therapy. Flat out, it works. It works at least as well as medication does for treating depression, and it appears to provide a degree of protection against relapse — something medication can't do.

✔ **Behavior therapy:** Studies have found that changing your behavior can also improve the way you feel and alleviate your depression. Behavior therapy focuses on helping you change behaviors (such as increasing your pleasurable activities and teaching you ways to solve problems). Most practitioners of behavior therapy also include cognitive techniques in their work. Many of these professionals call themselves cognitive-behavioral therapists.

✔ **Interpersonal therapy:** This type of therapy attempts to help people identify and modify problems in their relationships, both past and present. Considerable evidence supports the value of interpersonal therapy for decreasing depression. Like cognitive therapy, this approach has also been shown to alleviate depression about as well as medication. Sometimes this method of therapy delves into issues involving loss, grief, and major changes in a person's life, such as retirement or divorce. A fair portion of this approach also involves the relationship between the therapist and client (like learning to relate to the therapist in ways that may help you with other relationships), which a book can't provide.

Most people aren't aware that hundreds of different types of therapy exist. If you cast around, you may run into practitioners of psychoanalysis, hakomi therapy, eye movement desensitization reprocessing (popularly referred to as EMDR), client-centered therapy, transactional analysis, and Gestalt therapy, just to name a few. We fully believe that many of these therapies have value, and some may work for depression. However, the scientific literature on these other types of therapy as applied to depression is quite limited. We suggest that you start with therapies that have been fully established as effective.

Discovering who's who in psychotherapy

Most people don't realize that, in the majority of states, just about anyone can call himself or herself a therapist without getting into trouble with the authorities, because licensing laws typically don't cover the title *therapist*. Instead, states regulate specific professional titles and the right to practice psychotherapy or prescribe medications.

In the following list, we review the most common professional titles controlled by state professional licensing boards. We also describe the usual training required to obtain each type of professional license, although requirements vary slightly from state to state. You need to ask about a practitioner's specific training in particular types of psychotherapy, because not all professionals have received training in the types of psychotherapy that have been found effective for depression (which we outline in the preceding section).

✔ **Clinical psychologists:** To become a licensed clinical psychologist, an individual has to earn a doctorate degree in psychology. In addition, she must complete a year-long internship followed by one or two years of supervised postdoctoral training. Doctoral programs in psychology generally emphasize the science of human behavior and provide training in psychotherapies validated by research. Nevertheless, you need to check on a psychologist's expertise in cognitive-behavioral or interpersonal therapy before you commit to working on your depression with her.

✔ **Counselors:** Licensed, independent counselors have a master's degree and two years of post-graduate supervision. In a few cases, counselors may have only bachelor's degrees in education, psychology, or theology. *Pastoral counselors* have theological training in addition to training in counseling. Most counselors provide a range of psychotherapies. Inquire about their specific experience with the types of psychotherapy found to be successful for depression.

✔ **Psychiatrists:** Psychiatrists earn a medical degree and participate in a four-year residency program that trains them in the treatment and diagnosis of emotional disorders, including depression. Their training typically emphasizes biological treatments. Therefore, many psychiatrists strictly deal with medication management and/or alternative biological therapies, such as electroconvulsive shock therapy. However, some psychiatrists do receive extensive training in psychotherapy. If you're interested in obtaining psychotherapy, be sure to ask if the psychiatrist you're thinking about working with offers it.

✔ **Social workers:** Social workers sometimes go by various titles, such as *licensed social worker* and *independent social worker*. Folks who reach the most advanced levels of training receive the titles *qualified clinical social worker* and *diplomate in clinical social work*. To become a qualified clinical social worker, the applicant must have earned at least a master's degree in social work, worked two years under supervision beyond the master's degree, and passed a comprehensive national examination. Social workers provide a range of psychotherapies, although some of them focus on arranging social services and helping people access resources. A social worker's title doesn't necessarily indicate the extent of his psychotherapy training. So just ask to find out whether the social worker you're planning to work with offers psychotherapy and has been trained in therapies found effective for the treatment of depression.

Finding the right therapist for you

Some people take less time choosing a therapist than they do picking out the best cantaloupe at the grocery store. That's too bad, because the right therapist can help you recover and reach new levels of adjustment and well-being. And in the worst case, the wrong therapist can take your time and money, actually causing increased emotional distress.

Important issues to consider when you look for a therapist include

✔ **Finances:** Ask how much the therapist charges and whether your insurance covers that specific professional. Some insurance companies have lists of so-called preferred provider therapists they cover. Some policies allow you to see almost any licensed therapist, while others restrict access to a very narrow panel of providers. Though unusual, a few companies cover only psychotherapies known to be effective. Be sure to check your coverage rather than make an expensive mistake based on assumptions. Some people choose not to use insurance because they want to see a particular professional or have special concerns about privacy.

Investing money in therapy ultimately pays off in numerous, unexpected ways. For example, studies have shown that psychotherapy actually reduces medical doctor visits; it also appears to improve physical health in addition to mental health.

✔ **Reputation and recommendations:** Therapists can't provide you with the names of satisfied customers, because they're bound to respect confidentiality. However, you can inquire about therapists' reputations from other sources. Ask around. Talk to your friends and/or your family physician.

Beware of advertisements in the newspaper, television, or phone book: They *are not* especially reliable sources of information about therapists' reputations.

✔ **Scheduling:** Some therapists have extremely full practices with very limited options for appointment times. You may need to find someone who sees people in the evenings or on weekends. Be sure to ask what hours the therapist keeps.

✔ **Training and licensure:** We discuss the general training requirements for various licensed mental health professionals in the "Discovering who's who in psychotherapy" section, earlier in this chapter. Consider this entry on our list as a reminder to ask about training and experience in the therapies known to work for depression, such as cognitive therapy, behavior therapy, and interpersonal therapy. (For a definition of these therapies, check out the "Uncovering the effective therapies" section, earlier in this chapter.)

Do you have a good match with your therapist?

Most of the time when people choose a therapist, they feel a good connection, and they get better. Therapists generally are bright, kind, and skillful. However, therapists and clients sometimes just don't make a good match.

You may find that your therapist is a poor match for you. Maybe the therapist looks just like your ex-spouse, and every time you go to therapy, you feel a flood of painful memories. Or maybe you don't feel connected to your therapist for some reason you don't understand. The quality of the therapeutic relationship has been found to consistently predict good or bad therapy outcomes, so it's critical that you feel comfortable.

 Here are some questions you may want to ask yourself to help determine your comfort level after you see your therapist a few times:

✓ Do I feel like I can tell my therapist just about anything?

✓ Does it seem like my therapist cares about me?

✓ Does my therapist understand me?

✓ Does my therapist seem interested in my problems?

✓ Does my therapist hear what I'm trying to say?

✓ Do I trust my therapist?

✓ Is my therapist nonjudgmental and noncritical with me?

✓ Do I feel safe discussing my problems with my therapist?

If you answer any of the preceding questions with a strong "no," or you answer several of them without a clear "yes," discuss your concerns with your therapist. If you feel that you can't discuss these issues with your therapist, ask yourself why.

If you have good reasons for feeling so unsafe that you can't imagine speaking frankly, you probably need to search for another therapist. On the other hand, if your reticence comes from shyness or embarrassment, please realize that therapists are trained to hear your concerns, and you have an absolute right and need to express them.

How your therapist reacts to your concerns about the quality of your client-therapist relationship tells you if the relationship can be repaired. Following is an example of how a good therapist may respond to a client's concerns:

Client: I need to talk to you about something.

Therapist: Sure, what is it?

Client: I've been feeling like I can't be honest with you because I'm afraid you'll be critical.

Therapist: I'm glad you brought that up. Can you help me understand when it's felt like I've been critical of you?

Client: Well, last week I told you about my plans to look for another job and you said I shouldn't do it.

Therapist: That must have sounded like criticism, as if I wasn't supporting you.

Client: Yes, it did. It felt like you thought I was stupid.

Therapist: That must have felt awful. Can you think of any other reason I might have made that suggestion?

Client: No. Was there one?

Therapist: Well, yes. I've simply found that when people make major life decisions while they're in the throes of a major depression like you, they often regret their action later. It's just so hard to look at things objectively at times like this. On the other hand, I certainly want to explore your unhappiness at your job. Come to think of it, I probably didn't ask you enough about that. Would you like to tell me more now?

The exchange seems to work out fairly nicely, doesn't it? The therapist listens carefully to the client's concerns, acknowledges having failed to adequately explore the issue, and demonstrates interest in doing so. If your therapist responds to you in this manner, we suggest that you remain in therapy a little longer to see if the relationship can become more productive.

 But sometimes therapists have their own problems, and they don't respond very well to clients' concerns. Here's an example:

Client: I need to talk to you about something.

Therapist: Sure, what is it?

Client: I've been feeling like I can't be honest with you because I'm afraid you'll be critical.

Therapist: Well, I certainly don't think I've ever criticized you. What would make you think such a thing?

Client: Well, last week I told you about my plans to look for another job, and you said I shouldn't do it.

Therapist: That's because you're in no condition to be looking around for work. You're far too depressed to do something like that. You really thought I was criticizing you?

Client: Yes, I did. It felt like you thought I was stupid.

Therapist: That's ridiculous! You're obviously feeling overly defensive. We need to work on that.

Client: To be honest, I'm just not feeling heard by you.

Therapist: Well, you're wrong; I'm clearly listening to you.

In this case, the conversation does nothing to repair the strained relationship. The therapist reacts defensively and shows no support, empathy, or connection with the client. If your discussions with your therapist often sound like this one, you probably should consider going to another professional.

Talking to a Professional about Antidepressant Medication

The decision of whether to use medication for your depression is a complex one. If you opt for antidepressant drugs, you still need to know who to get them from. A variety of different professionals prescribe medications for depression.

Professionals who prescribe most medications

As you may imagine, physicians prescribe most antidepressant medications. Two types of physicians prescribe these medications far more frequently than other physicians:

✔ **Primary care physicians:** These physicians are the ones most people go to for their routine care, such as annual physicals and treatment for colds and flu. This group includes specialists, such as family practice physicians, internists, geriatric physicians, and sometimes even gyne-cologists. Talking to your family physician about your symptoms of depression can be a reason-able way to start your treatment.

In fact, you may be surprised to know that pri-mary care physicians write more than 60 per-cent of the prescriptions given for emotional disorders. Nevertheless, if your depression is quite severe or complicated by other problems, such as anxiety or substance abuse, you need to consult a psychiatrist.

Before you ask for antidepressant medication from your primary care physician, be sure to find out whether your doctor is comfortable with these medications. Some general practi-tioners have considerable training in using medications to treat emotional disorders, while others know relatively little about this specific area.

✔ **Psychiatrists:** Keep in mind that psychiatrists receive more extensive training in the biological treatments of depression than any other pre-scribing group of professionals. (See the "Discovering who's who in psychotherapy" section, earlier in this chapter, for more info.) In addition, they regularly see patients with depression and other emotional disorders. Thus, they have considerable experience with the tricky side effects and drug-interaction issues involved with antidepressant medication.

Occasional prescribers

A few professionals, in addition to physicians, are allowed to prescribe antidepressant medication and do so from time to time. However, this group of pro-fessionals typically has relatively less training in emo-tional problems like depression.

You're probably only going to want to seek a member of the following groups out if your depression is fairly mild and hasn't been a chronic, long-term condition:

- **Nurse practitioners and physician assistants:** A majority of states allow these professionals to prescribe antidepressant medication in addition to other medications. Most of these practitioners have quite limited training in the treatment of emotional problems such as depression. If your depression isn't severe or complicated by the presence of other emotional problems (such as physical maladies, substance abuse, or suicidal thoughts), you may consider obtaining antidepressant medication from these midlevel providers.

- **Pharmacists:** In several states, pharmacists are lobbying for the right to prescribe certain types of medication. Usually this privilege involves collaboration with a primary care physician. Pharmacists also have quite limited training in the treatment of emotional problems, but you can consider obtaining your medication from a pharmacist if you have a mild, uncomplicated form of depression. (See Chapter 5 for more information about the different types of depression.)

Mental health professionals who generally don't prescribe

The vast majority of mental health professionals don't prescribe antidepressant medication. Although they may have received some training and education about the use and effects of these drugs, they don't prescribe. See the "Discovering who's who in psychotherapy" section, earlier in this chapter, for more information on the training of the following professionals:

- ✔ **Counselors:** Though frequently well trained in psychotherapy, counselors don't currently prescribe medications in any state.

- ✔ **Psychologists:** Most psychologists don't prescribe medications of any kind. However, a small number of psychologists in the armed services and Guam who have considerable additional training in psychopharmacology prescribe medications for emotional disorders only. Legislation was passed in New Mexico (and is pending in many other states) to enable more psychologists, following additional training, to ultimately prescribe these medications (for emotional disorders only). These practitioners recommend a complete physical examination to rule out any possible physical causes of your depression prior to prescribing an antidepressant.

- ✔ **Social workers:** Many social workers have received excellent training in psychotherapy, but at this time they're not allowed to prescribe medications in any state.

If you decide to take medication and also receive psychotherapy from another provider, encourage your therapist to communicate with the health care professional who is prescribing your medication. Communication ensures that both professionals are working on the same page.

Tired and stressed? You must be depressed!

While we were writing another one of our *For Dummies* books, *Overcoming Anxiety For Dummies* (Wiley Publishing, Inc.), Laura was also working as a clinical psychologist at a local hospital. In the midst of writing the book and fulfilling her duties at the hospital, she visited her primary care physician and complained of fatigue. The doctor asked about her stress, which Laura had to acknowledge was fairly high. The doctor suggested that she was depressed. Laura said, "No, I'm quite sure I'm not depressed." She explained that she was still interested in things and didn't have any pessimistic thinking about the future. The doctor stated that mental health professionals are the worst at diagnosing themselves. Laura still protested, but the doctor insisted that she was in denial. Laura reluctantly went home with a prescription for an antidepressant medication.

The next day, the doctor's office called with the results of Laura's blood test. It showed that she was actually suffering from hypothyroidism, which fully explained her fatigue. Laura tossed the antidepressant prescription into the trash after discussing the findings with the doctor. Had the doctor known to inquire about other symptoms of depression, such as low self-worth, guilt, loss of interest in pleasurable activities, and so on, she would have realized that the cause was more likely physical in nature.

Laura's example describes one of the problems you can encounter when seeking treatment from your primary care physician. Generally, a brief ten-minute office visit proves insufficient for diagnosing emotional disorders; the short visit can actually lead to an erroneous initial impression. But don't get us wrong. Your primary care physician is usually a great place to start for most physical problems and sometimes for emotional difficulties as well. More and more primary care physicians are now receiving training in the recognition and treatment of depression.

Chapter 8

Ten Signs That You Need Professional Help

Some people find that self-help is all they need. However, no self-help book is intended to completely replace professional help. We hope you understand that seeking a mental health professional's assistance is a reasonable choice, not a sign of weakness.

This chapter tells you how to know if you should consider professional assistance for yourself or someone you care about. It isn't always an obvious decision, so we give you a list of indicators. And if you still aren't sure, you can always talk with your primary care doctor, who should be able to help you decide.

Having Suicidal Thoughts or Plans

If you find yourself thinking about harming yourself, get help now. Take these thoughts very seriously. Call the national suicide hotline at: <tel>**1-800-SUICIDE** (1-800-784-2433). Or call a friend. If your thoughts become overwhelming, call <tel>911 and get to an emergency room. Help is available. And when you do access professional help, be honest about your thoughts; hold nothing back.

Feeling Hopeless

From time to time, everyone feels defeated. But if you begin to feel hopeless about getting better, thinking that the future looks bleak and you can't do much to change it, get professional help. Feelings of hopelessness put you at greater risk for suicide. But you need to know that you *can* feel better. Let others help you.

Handling Anxiety and Depression

You may be experiencing depression mixed with anxiety if you find yourself having some of the following symptoms:

- ✔ Feeling sad most of the day
- ✔ Losing interest or pleasure in activities
- ✔ Changes in weight
- ✔ Changes in your sleep patterns and habits
- ✔ Feeling keyed up or slowed down
- ✔ Feeling worthless

> ✔ Feeling excessively guilty
>
> ✔ Poor concentration
>
> ✔ Thoughts of death

If you do have anxiety and depression, seek professional help. Anxiety and depression are treatable conditions. Having the energy to fight both can be hard.

Trying and Trying and Trying

So you read the book and gave your best shot at overcoming anxiety, but for whatever reason, it just hasn't worked. That's okay. Don't get more anxious because you didn't get rid of your worry and stress. Something else may be going on. Get an experienced mental health professional to help you figure out the next step.

Struggling at Home

You're anxious. The anxiety causes you to be irritable, jumpy, and upset. You hold it together at work and with strangers, but you take it out on the people you care about most, your family. Then you feel guilty, which increases your anxiety. If this sounds like you, a professional may help you decrease the tension at home and ease your pathway to finding peace.

Dealing with Major Problems at Work

Maybe you have no one at home to take your anxiety out on, or home is your haven away from stress. If that's the case, work stress may overwhelm you. If you find your anxiety exploding at work, consider professional help.

First, anxiety sometimes causes irritability and moodiness with coworkers or bosses, which can cause plenty of trouble. Anxiety can also rob you of your short-term memory and make it difficult to focus or make decisions. So if anxiety affects your job performance, get help before you hit the unemployment line.

Suffering from Severe Obsessions or Compulsions

Obsessive Compulsive Disorder (OCD) can be serious. See Chapter 1 for more information about OCD. The problem is that people with the disorder often don't seek help until unwanted thoughts or repetitive actions overtake their lives. Most people with OCD need professional help. If you or someone you love has more than mild OCD, get professional help.

Understanding Post-Traumatic Stress Disorder

You feel agitated and keyed up. Were you also exposed to a traumatic event in which

  ✔ You felt helpless and afraid?

  ✔ You tried not to think about it?

  ✔ Thoughts and images of the event kept on popping up in spite of your efforts not to think about it?

If so, you may have *Post-Traumatic Stress Disorder* (PTSD). See Chapter 1 for a complete description of PTSD. An experienced professional can probably best treat PTSD. Many people with PTSD try to tough it out and live life less fully because of their stubbornness.

Going through Sleepless Nights

Is anxiety keeping you awake? That's quite common. But too many sleepless nights make it hard to function and make it more difficult to help yourself in the fight against anxiety. If you sleep poorly night after night and awake tired, check it out with a professional. You may be experiencing depression along with anxiety.

Getting High

Sure, a beer or three can sooth a soul, but excessive drinking or drug abuse is a common problem among people with anxiety disorders. It makes sense; anxious feelings are uncomfortable. What begins as an innocent attempt at feeling better can become another big problem later on. If you find yourself using too much alcohol or another drug to calm your feelings, get professional help before your crutch turns into an addiction.

Finding Help

In these days of managed care, you may not always have as much freedom to consult any professional you want. However, whether you receive a restricted list of professionals from your insurance company or not, it's still a good idea to check out one or more of the following:

✔ Ask your insurance company or the state licensing board for the specific profession or license of the referred professional.

✔ Ask your friends if they know of someone that they had a good experience with.

✔ Ask your primary care doctor. Family physicians usually have a good idea about excellent referrals for various types of problems.

✔ Talk to the professional before making an appointment. Ask about experience with treating anxiety and what approach he takes. Ask whether you will receive a scientifically verified approach for dealing with anxiety.

✔ Call the psychology department of your local college or university. Sometimes psychology departments have referral lists.

✔ Call your state psychological, psychiatric, or counseling association. Or check out national consumer organizations.

Diet, Health, & Fitness Titles from For Dummies

For Dummies books help keep you healthy and fit. Whatever
your health & fitness needs, turn to Dummies books first.

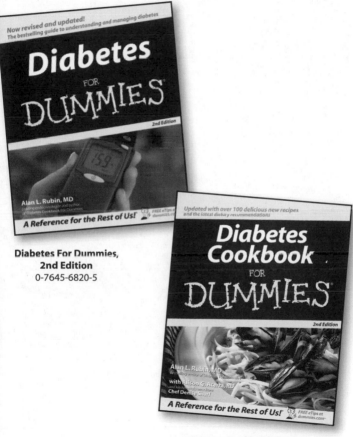

**Diabetes For Dummies,
2nd Edition**
0-7645-6820-5

**Diabetes Cookbook For Dummies,
2nd Edition**
0-7645-8450-2

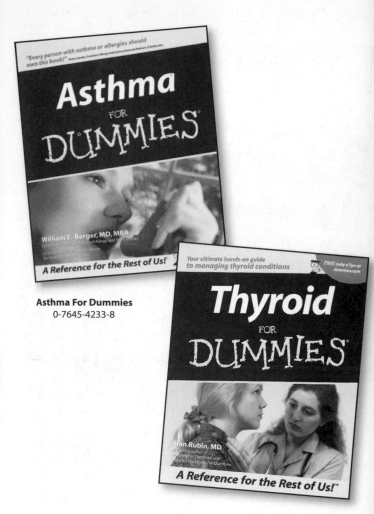

Asthma For Dummies
0-7645-4233-8

Thyroid For Dummies
0-7645-5385-2

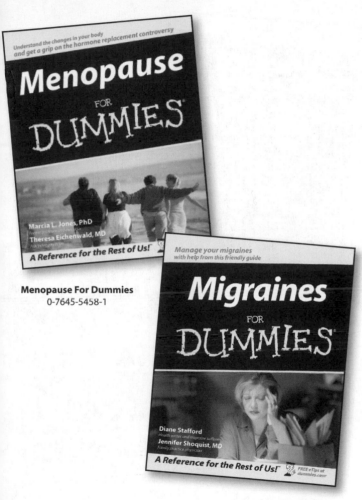

Menopause For Dummies
0-7645-5458-1

Migraines For Dummies
0-7645-5485-9

**Overcoming Anxiety
For Dummies**
0-7645-5447-6

Depression For Dummies
0-7645-3900-0